NONE OF US
IS AS GOOD
AS ALL OF US

NONE OF US IS AS GOOD AS ALL OF US

HOW McDONALD'S PROSPERS BY EMBRACING INCLUSION AND DIVERSITY

PATRICIA SOWELL HARRIS

WILEY

John Wiley & Sons, Inc.

Published by John Wiley & Sons, Inc., Hoboken, New Jersey.
Published simultaneously in Canada.

For general information on our other products and services or for technical support, please contact our Customer Care Department within the United States at (800) 762-2974, outside the United States at (317) 572-3993 or fax (317) 572-4002.

Wiley also publishes its books in a variety of electronic formats. Some content that appears in print may not be available in electronic books. For more information about Wiley products, visit our web site at www.wiley.com.

Library of Congress Cataloging-in-Publication Data:

Harris, Patricia Sowell.
    None of us is as good as all of us: how McDonald's prospers by embracing inclusion and diversity / by Patricia Sowell Harris.
        p.   cm.
    Includes index.
    ISBN 978-0-470-49932-0 (cloth)
    1.   McDonald's Corporation—Management. 2.   Diversity in the workplace.   I. Title.
    TX945.5.M33H37 2009
    331.11'43—dc22
                                                                    2009031721

Printed in the United States of America

10 9 8 7 6 5 4 3 2 1

This book is dedicated to the hundreds of thousands of my colleagues who bring diversity to life at McDonald's every day . . . to my late father and mother, who made me who I am and would be proud of who I have become . . . and to my son, Dwayne, and granddaughter, Cydnii, who represent the promise of a better future.

CONTENTS

FOREWORD

$\mathcal{M}$cDonald's has an unwavering commitment to inclusion and diversity in our workforce, among our franchisees, and with our suppliers—in the United States and everywhere else in the world where we do business. I'm proud that our company values diversity so highly, and I am delighted that Pat Harris has taken on the task of sharing the evolution of diversity at McDonald's because it is a story that all of us can take to heart and learn from.

The first lesson that struck me in our story is that the road to becoming a diverse company is not a straight one. There are many bumps and potholes to negotiate and twists and turns that can, and sometimes do, take you off the right path. Like anyone, we have had our share of barriers and obstacles, but we have learned to keep our eye on the goal and persist through the hard times.

We have also learned that diversity is a sound business strategy—the smart thing to do if you wish to serve a diverse customer base. Frankly, there is nothing wrong with combining altruism with a very practical approach to diversity, and for those who say that it is easier to embrace diversity when you are the biggest and best in your industry, I would argue that the cause and effect is just the opposite. I believe that our diversity strategies are among the business practices that have helped us to become the acknowledged leader of the quick-service restaurant industry.

And, finally, as Pat makes clear in these pages, inclusion and diversity are not a destination you reach, they are a journey you take.

There might be many milestones you pass along the way to mark your progress, but the real benefits come from a constant effort to do things better tomorrow than you do them today. You might achieve diversity goals from a numbers standpoint but still miss the mark, because the true measurement of your success is how you leverage diversity for the benefit of your business and your people.

As McDonald's CEO, I am proud to introduce this book to you, and I do so with a salute to all the women and men within our system who have made such an encouraging and inspirational story possible.

—Jim Skinner
McDonald's Chief Executive Officer

MESSAGE

*A*s a long-time franchisee and member of the McDonald's "system," I was delighted to learn that Pat Harris was writing this book on the evolution of diversity within McDonald's. I know from firsthand experience that the opportunities McDonald's has provided to people of all races and ethnic backgrounds have been extraordinary and that this is a remarkable story well worth sharing with the rest of the world.

As the chair of Ronald McDonald House Charities (RMHC), I was even more pleased when Pat told me she has decided to donate all profits from this book to our organization. I am happy to accept this truly generous gesture on behalf of all the children around the world who benefit from RMHC programs.

As you might know, RMHC is a public charity founded in 1984 in memory of Ray Kroc, McDonald's founder. In partnership with our local chapters, we have donated more than $460 million to date to programs that improve the lives of children and their families in neighborhoods worldwide.

Perhaps our most recognized initiative is our Ronald McDonald House program, which operates throughout the world, providing comfort to families with seriously ill children. The first Ronald McDonald House opened in Philadelphia in 1974, and today there are more than 285 Ronald McDonald Houses in 30 countries.

McDonald's commitment to be a good neighbor and contribute to the communities that support our business is based upon the same values and principles that underlie our commitment to diversity. Pat sums it up aptly by using Ray Kroc's own words as the title of this book—"None of us is as good as all of us."

—Linda Dunham
Chair, Ronald McDonald House Charities

Timeline: Key Dates in McDonald's Diversity History

1957	June Martino is elected Secretary/Treasurer of Franchise Realty Corp., which becomes part of McDonald's Corporation in 1960.
1960	Lillian McMahon becomes the first woman franchisee of a McDonald's restaurant.
1966	June Martino is the second woman allowed on the floor of the NYSE (Queen Elizabeth was the first) when McDonald's stock is listed.
1968	Herman Petty of Chicago becomes McDonald's first African American restaurant owner. For the first time, women are allowed to work as crew members at company-owned restaurants.
1969	June Martino retires and becomes honorary lifetime member of McDonald's Board of Directors. Bob Beavers joins McDonald's licensing department to recruit African American franchisees.
1970	The Black McDonald's Operators Association (BMOA) is formed in Chicago, electing Ed Wimp as its president.
1971	Women are introduced to company-owned restaurant management ranks. Henry Garcia becomes first Hispanic franchisee in Los Angeles.
1972	The Chicago BMOA holds its first convention.

1973	McDonald's begins its formal association with Burrell Advertising, an African American marketing firm founded by Tom Burrell.
1974	McDonald's begins its annual Employee Satisfaction/ Commitment surveys.
1975	Ted Tongson becomes first Asian American franchisee in Paris, Texas. Sandy Brooks named first female Regional Vice President.
1976	The National Black McDonald's Operators Association (NBMOA) is formed in Philadelphia, electing Ralph Kelly president.
1977	McDonald's "Big Brother" mentoring program for African American employees is launched at a symposium in Atlanta. The McDonald's Hispanic Operators Association (MHOA) is formed and holds its first official meeting in Albuquerque, NM.
1979	Dr. Ron Brown, an African American consultant, is retained by McDonald's to assist in our affirmative action programs. Women's Career Development training classes are launched.
1980	McDonald's hires African American Mel Hopson to head Affirmative Action department.
1982	McDonald's creates "McJobs" program to hire and develop disabled employees.
1984	Bob Beavers becomes first African American named to McDonald's Board of Directors. Ron Damper becomes McDonald's first national African American supplier, providing tea to local restaurants.
1985	Franchisee Richard Castro launches the Hispanic American Commitment to Education Resources (HACER) scholarship fund.

1986	McDonald's introduces McMasters, a program to recruit older workers.
1988	Women Operators Network (WON) is formed, electing Darlene McKeller as its first president.
1989	McDonald's is one of the founding members of the Women's Foodservice Forum.
1990	Terry Savage, nationally renowned financial expert, becomes first woman elected to McDonald's Board of Directors. McDonald's Women's Leadership Network (WLN) for women employees is formed.
1991	Mike Sewell, a McDonald's crew member with Down Syndrome, appears in an inspiring Super Bowl commercial.
1992	Rodney King riots in Los Angeles cause $2 billion in damage but leave McDonald's restaurants virtually untouched.
1994	McDonald's WON receives the Catalyst Award for advancing women and promoting leadership within the organization. The WLN holds its first national conference for women employees.
1996	Enrique Hernandez, Jr., former chairman and CEO of Inter-Con Security Systems, is the first Hispanic elected to McDonald's Board of Directors.
1998	Walter Massey, African American then-president of Morehouse College, is elected to McDonald's Board of Directors.
1999	National Leadership Council of franchisees is formally established, including Executive Committee representation from each owner/operator diversity association. Ed Sanchez is named president of the Latin America Group. Jeanne Jackson, former CEO of Walmart.com (now

president of Direct to Consumer for Nike.com), is elected to McDonald's Board of Directors.

2000 Pat Harris is named to head Diversity Department, replacing Mel Hopson, who retires. McDonald's is named *Fortune* magazine's Most Admired Company for Social Responsibility.

2001 Hispanic Gloria Santona becomes General Counsel of McDonald's Corporation. McDonald's USA names Hispanic Henry Gonzalez president of East Division, Hispanic Ralph Alvarez president of Central Division, and African American Don Thompson president of West Division.

2002 African American Bill Lamar becomes head of U.S. Marketing for McDonald's USA. Jack Greenberg, McDonald's CEO, is presented the Trailblazer Award by the Women's Foodservice Forum. McDonald's launches its first "Diversity Best Practice Symposium," sharing its diversity programs with 39 outside corporations.

2003 Jan Fields is named president of McDonald's USA Central Division as Ralph Alvarez becomes U.S. Chief Operating Officer. Reggie Webb, African American owner/operator, is elected chairman of McDonald's National Leadership Council. African American John Rogers, founder and CEO of Ariel Capital Management (now Ariel Investments), is elected to McDonald's Board of Directors. The Asian McDonald's Operator Association (AMOA) helps establish the Asian & Pacific Islander American Scholarship Fund (APIASF). *Fortune* magazine names McDonald's the "Best Place for Minorities to Work."

2004 McDonald's forms Diversity Advisory Council, headed by Pat Harris, Chief Diversity Officer. Ralph Alvarez becomes president of McDonald's USA. McDonald's enables domestic partners to be eligible for its benefits package. *Fortune* magazine names McDonald's the "Best Place for Minorities to Work."

2005   Karen King is named president of McDonald's USA East Division. Mary Dillon becomes McDonald's Global Chief Marketing Officer. McDonald's Gay, Lesbian and Allies Network (MGLAN) employee network is established.

2006   McDonald's receives the U.S. EEOC "Freedom to Compete" award for its diversity and inclusion initiatives. Ralph Alvarez is named McDonald's President and COO and Don Thompson becomes president of McDonald's USA. Pat Harris is honored with the National Restaurant Association's Salute to Excellence Award. Sheila Penrose, then-president of The Penrose Group (now non-executive Chairman of the Board), is elected to McDonald's Board of Directors.

2007   McDonald's European Women's Leadership Network holds its first meeting.

2008   Ralph Alvarez is elected to McDonald's Board of Directors. McDonald's Asia/Pacific Women's Network holds its first meeting. Susan Arnold, then-president of Global Business Units of The Procter & Gamble Company (now on special assignment for the CEO), is elected to McDonald's Board of Directors J.C. Gonzalez-Mendez is named president, McDonald's Latin America. Jose Armario is promoted to group president, McDonald's Canada and Latin America.

2009   McDonald's selected by *LATINA Style* magazine as one of the Top Twelve Companies of the Year, named one of the best companies for Latinas to work for in the United States.

1

Welcome to McDonald's

*W*elcome to McDonald's.

That's a familiar phrase to our customers. They hear it repeated more than 58 million times every day when they enter the Golden Arches in one of our 32,000 restaurants around the world. And that's also the spirit of inclusion we extend to the 1.6 million members of the McDonald's family—be they franchisees, restaurant workers, suppliers, or employees. Our welcome is inclusive and sincere because we know the diversity of our people helps us satisfy the world's most diverse customer base.

And that's the McDonald's I'd like to welcome you to as we look at the evolution of inclusion and diversity under the Golden Arches and how our commitment to those principles has contributed to the success of our business.

McDonald's has been widely recognized as one of the most successful companies in providing opportunities for a wide diversity of people—from the crew rooms in our restaurants to the board-room for the corporation. Our commitment to diversity extends beyond our own employees to our franchisees and their employees and our suppliers and their employees as well.

This multifaceted and integrated approach to welcoming people has become an integral part of the McDonald's business model—the so-called "secret sauce" behind our growth as one of the world's most recognized brands. While diversity at McDonald's is all about the business, our efforts have also resulted in numerous honors from outside organizations—including twice being voted by our peers as the Best Company for Diversity in *Fortune* magazine.

The numbers that people rely upon to make such judgments are strong, as you would expect, even though they reflect a direction, rather than a destination. As of January 1, 2009, our McDonald's workforce—from the crew members in our restaurants through our CEO—is comprised of 62 percent women, 35 percent Hispanics, 20 percent African Americans, 5 percent Asians, and 2 percent Native Americans. Many of those workers are holding their very first jobs, representing the launching pad for their careers at McDonald's, in the restaurant industry, or in virtually every other walk of life.

Small Part of the Story

But these numbers are only a small part of the story because we moved beyond simply counting heads a long time ago. Today, we are intent upon making heads count. So, at McDonald's, our definition of *diversity* includes a broad mix of different ideas, opinions, backgrounds, and life experiences in addition to the traditional measures like race and gender. That's how we make diversity an active, living part of our business strategies at McDonald's. Maintaining a diverse and inclusive workforce is certainly the right and proper thing to do, but we have long maintained that it is also the smart thing to do.

Any company that hopes to serve a diverse customer base across the United States, and around the world, must reflect that same diversity in the restaurants, where we meet our customers face to face, and throughout our organization, where we design our products and services with the distinct wants and needs of our customers in mind. And our business results reflect the validity of mirroring our customers throughout our system very clearly.

McDonald's has grown to include more than 32,000 restaurants in 118 countries around the world—nearly 14,000 of them in the United States alone—as of the beginning of 2009. We serve more than 58 million customers every single day around the world. Our annual sales at both franchise and company-owned restaurants amounted to more than $70 billion in 2008, producing $6.4 billion in operating income. By any yardstick, McDonald's is far and away the market leader in the Quick Service Restaurant category—a segment that we virtually created since we began operations more than five decades ago.

As McDonald's Global Chief Inclusion and Diversity Officer, I am as proud of our record as any of the 1.6 million people in our global family. But I must also tell you, in all honesty, that it wasn't always this way.

Societal Attitudes

When we were founded in 1955 by Ray Kroc, McDonald's reflected the attitudes of U.S. society in general. In that post-World War II environment, race and gender equality in the workforce were unheard of and talked about very little. It was very unusual when women, as epitomized by Rosie the Riveter, took on many factory and industrial jobs during the war. But, when the war was over, most women moved back into the home and made way for the veterans to return to their jobs. McDonald's itself didn't even allow women to work in our restaurants until the mid-1960s.

So, when pent-up societal issues in the United States began to erupt in the 1960s, McDonald's executives—like everyone else in the corporate business world—realized that they had new challenges to face. It has not been a smooth road to get where we are today, and there surely are still bumps to overcome.

However, there were several factors that helped McDonald's appreciate the value of diversity that came into play throughout its evolution. I will mention them briefly here because they represent the theme of this historical look at diversity development, and they will come into sharper focus throughout this book. It is my opinion that they are replicable by any other organization that is struggling to embrace diversity today, whether your efforts are just beginning, or started earlier and are now stalled, or are still on your organizational "to do" list.

Support From the Top

The first essential element is a strong and unwavering commitment to diversity from senior management.

Ray Kroc created a unique organization when he started McDonald's in the 1950s, using a business model that seemed downright radical at the time because he set up McDonald's like a three-legged stool, with the legs of the stool representing the franchisees, suppliers, and company. Each leg of the stool had to prosper for the others to succeed, thereby creating a partnership of interests that required the entire system to work together.

Kroc used to say, "None of us is as good as all of us," and, while it was originally aimed at the way McDonald's three-legged stool had to operate, it was prophetic in the way it came to apply to our diversity efforts as well.

Above all else, Kroc was interested in selling hamburgers, and when it became clear to him and to Fred Turner, his right-hand man, that we needed African American, Hispanic, and Asian entrepreneurs to help sell more hamburgers in minority communities, that was the approach they took. Like everything Kroc and Turner took on, they did so enthusiastically, and McDonald's top management has reflected that commitment through the years. Leadership from the top is critically important in embracing diversity.

Training Is Key

The second important element is training and education.

This was also a well-ingrained attribute at McDonald's from the very beginning. We hired so many high school kids that we quickly became America's favorite first job. That meant we had to train our people in basic restaurant operations—and, indeed, in fundamental on-the-job behaviors and attitudes—to get them up and running.

In addition, we needed to train our owner/operators and store managers in advanced restaurant operations—how to run a restaurant "the McDonald's way," if you will—and that meant creating Hamburger University, our state-of-the-art training center, as well as regional training centers. So, from the early days, McDonald's was a company that understood the value of training and used training to accomplish our business goals.

Training became one of the important tools we used to make diversity work at McDonald's Corporation as well. We discovered that bringing people in the front door was the easy part. But, without training to develop corporate survival skills, those same people would soon walk out the back door. So we trained our women and minority employees to understand the corporate environment and develop strategies for personal success. We also trained their managers and supervisors so they could learn how to understand and manage a diverse workforce.

That's why our diversity training and education continues to this day—it reflects all that we have learned and addresses the barriers that we still need to overcome.

Networks Are Invaluable

Finally, the third element that fosters a diverse workforce is employee networks.

Networks are established in our home office and in every region of the country and most of the world to foster relationships and career development opportunities through meetings and seminars that enhance our employees' development and promotional opportunities. We patterned our employee networks after the associations that our minority and women owner/operator members formed to leverage their own interests, like the National Black McDonald's Operators Association, the Women Operators Network, the McDonald's Hispanic Operators Association, and the Asian McDonald's Operators Association.

Today, there are employee networks for Women, African Americans, Hispanics, Asians, Gays and Lesbians, Young Professionals, and Working Mothers, and they keep our people connected, in touch with potential mentors, and on top of career development opportunities.

Management support, training and education, and networks are the three building blocks for an effective diversity initiative in any company, and my own personal career reflects all three of those elements as well. It's how I came to be what I am today.

Telling Our Story

I am the last of 11 children raised in a farming family in McBee, South Carolina, and my aspiration as I was growing up was to be a secretary for a major corporation in New York City. That goal turned out to be a launching pad for where I ultimately wound up.

Today, in my role as Vice President and Global Chief Diversity Officer at McDonald's Corporation, I work closely with the company's senior officers, and, for some time, I worked every day in the very same office where Ray Kroc, the founder of McDonald's, once worked. There isn't a day that goes by without my taking a moment to consider the awesome capability people have to grow into greater responsibilities when they are given a chance.

It has been an amazing journey—for me and for McDonald's—and that's why I have decided to tell this story, this evolutionary tale of how a little hamburger company grew to be one of the most diverse and inclusive business organizations in the world. It's not only a fascinating history, but I believe others can learn a great deal from McDonald's experience.

To tell this story, I have interviewed dozens of people who have been an integral part of McDonald's diversity history—from past senior management to my colleagues today, from pioneering owner/operators to current leaders of our operator networks, from women and minority suppliers for our restaurants to the consultants who helped establish our original training programs.

Hear Their Voices

Our success in building our record of diversity is really the result of the contributions of all our people. That's why you will hear their voices throughout these pages—because I believe it's most credible to tell our story from the perspective of the people who made it all happen.

I have also relied upon the accounts of McDonald's early history in some excellent books, including *Grinding It Out* by Ray Kroc himself, *Behind the Arches* by John Love, *McDonald's @ 50*, which was published by the company in 2005 to commemorate our first 50 years in business, and *Standing Up & Standing Out* by Roland Jones, one of our pioneer African American employees and, later, a successful franchisee.

And, of course, I have lived this history personally for the past three decades.

My part in this story is simple. I am one of literally tens of thousands of people who have been touched by the opportunities that McDonald's provides to its people, whether they are employees, franchisees, or suppliers. This organization has understood from its very beginning that the surest path to success is to provide opportunities to help people reach their own potential—and I am certainly no exception.

A Farmer's Daughter

I was born Patricia Janice Sowell in 1947. In that small South Carolina town of McBee, my father raised watermelons, strawberries, and sweet potatoes as well as 11 children—five girls and six boys. I was 14 years old when he died in 1961. My mother was a self-educated woman who didn't even graduate from high school, but she worked as a practical nurse as well as a substitute teacher at the little school in McBee whenever the principal called.

I still remember vividly, when I was in high school, they hired the first typing teacher my school had ever had and purchased all these great typewriters for the students to practice our skills. I loved to type, I became very good at it, and I remember thinking, "Wow, I want to be a corporate secretary when I grow up." I even put that in my high school yearbook.

For some reason, all my brothers left the farm and moved to Philadelphia when they grew up, and all my sisters moved to New York. As a result, I visited those big cities many times during summer vacations to baby-sit for their children—my little nieces and nephews—and I had already decided that New York was going to be the place for me. So, when I graduated from high school at the age of 16, I immediately moved to New York and enrolled in Brown's Business School for a year. After working for a couple of different little companies, I landed a job with General Electric Company as a secretary and stayed there for six years.

On to Chicago

I moved to Chicago in 1976 and initially worked at a job at CNA Insurance Company as a secretary for the senior vice president of Human Resources, although he left the company just a couple of months after I arrived. After a short stint at a Chicago insurance brokerage firm, I interviewed at McDonald's and got a job as an administrative assistant to Noel Kaplan, one of our corporate attorneys in the Legal department.

The very process of being hired gave me an immediate insight into McDonald's style of doing business because Noel interviewed me on a Friday, offered me a job on the spot, and wanted me to start Monday. After I explained that I had to give my current employer time to find a replacement, he said, "Well, okay, give them a week's notice, and then you start."

All during this time, I had been pursuing a college degree, attending classes part-time at Queensborough College and then

York College while I lived and worked in New York, and then at Roosevelt University in Chicago. So, when I started work at McDonald's in February of 1976, I thought the job would just be something to tide me over until I got my degree in Personnel Management a couple of years down the road.

But, like many people who originally considered McDonald's a temporary detour in life, the little job that I didn't think would amount to anything has turned into a career of more than three decades, making a living has been transformed into building a life, and past successes continually evolve into future challenges.

But I'm getting ahead of myself. To understand the evolution of diversity at McDonald's, you need to know more about where the McDonald's "three-legged stool" system started and how our very structure helped us overcome the barriers to diversity that face every organization in the United States today.

Let's start at the beginning.

―――――――――

Lessons Learned

As we proceed through this book, I plan to highlight what I consider a big idea—one of the key lessons we learned—at the end of each chapter. I hope these lessons will serve as a guideline for others who are interested in learning from McDonald's experience and fostering a culture of diversity within their own organizations.

So, the first key lesson, right off the bat, addresses the misperception that diversity is a goal that stands apart from a company's profitability. In our experience, the two concepts go hand in hand.

In the opening pages, I detail McDonald's global scope and outstanding business results as well as our diversity accomplishments, and I did both for a reason: Our success in becoming a diverse and inclusive company is one of the key factors that has driven our positive results over the years.

You will see how this plays out through the course of the book, but the reasons are simple.

First, people like doing business with other people like themselves. This is just plain common sense, and all the studies show it to be true. So, when your employees and franchisees mirror the communities they serve, your customers can count on seeing friendly faces to serve them behind the counter and in the drive-thru window, or however you interface with your own customers.

Second, as you build a cadre of diverse people within your own company, you enhance your ability to understand your customers and gain insights into how you relate with them. In our case, our diversity includes our franchisees, our suppliers, and our employees—so, the more diverse we are, the better we can profit from our ability to have insights into what our consumers expect from us.

And, finally, as you increase the critical mass of diversity within your own ranks, you build a broader and deeper pool of talent to draw from in building your management team. No single group of people has a monopoly on good leadership and bright minds, so the wider you cast your net, the more people with great potential you are likely to attract to your organization.

I mention the power of diversity to improve your business results because I have seen too many companies approach their own practices from the more narrow perspective that diversity is "the right thing to do."

It is the right thing to do; there's no doubt about it. But, if your only goal is to feel better about yourself and your organization, you will find you are missing out on the full benefits of building and maintaining a diverse workforce to enhance your business success.

2

In the Beginning

*T*here really was a person named McDonald who started McDonald's. There were two of them, in fact—brothers Richard and Maurice or, as they were known to all of their friends, Dick and Mac.

Their story begins in the late 1940s, when the McDonald brothers were searching for a way to improve their little drive-in restaurant business in San Bernardino, California. Rather than tinker with the business, which was bringing in a very comfortable $200,000 yearly (about $1.7 million in today's dollars), they invented an entirely new concept for a restaurant based upon speedy service, low prices, and big volume.

They did away with carhops in favor of self-service at the counter. They ditched their 25-item barbecue menu in favor of a limited menu of just nine items: hamburger, cheeseburger, three soft-drink flavors, milk, coffee, potato chips, and pie. French fries and milkshakes were added soon after they opened their newly formatted restaurant.

They also reengineered their stainless steel kitchen to accommodate mass production and high-speed delivery with assembly-line procedures. And to bring in the volume needed to sustain this production, they slashed the price of their hamburger in half—from a competitive 30 cents to an unbelievably low 15 cents.

The new McDonald's reopened in December of 1948 and business took a while to build. However, it eventually became clear that the brothers had captured the spirit of a newly mobile and prosperous post-war America, and, by the 1950s, their little hamburger stand enjoyed annual revenues of $350,000, almost double the volume of their previous drive-in business at the same location. It was not unusual for as many as 150 customers to be crowded around the tiny hamburger stand waiting to be served during peak lunch-time periods.

As word of their success began to spread, the two brothers made a few half-hearted attempts to franchise their operation. For a thousand dollars, they would sell people the McDonald's name and a basic description of their Speedy Service System and send a counterman named Art Bender out for a couple of weeks to get their restaurant started. But the brothers were quite comfortable with their local success and not really interested in going through all the time and the trouble it would take to try and create a national chain of restaurants.

But then Ray Kroc came to visit their restaurant in 1954 and everything changed. The fast-food industry was about to take off.

A Born Salesman

Kroc was a 52-year-old milkshake machine salesman when he founded the company that revolutionized the way the world eats. He was a salesman through and through—he had sold paper cups to sidewalk vendors, he'd taken a fling at Florida real estate, and, finally, he had become the exclusive distributor for the "Multimixer" milkshake machine. A dreamer who thought big, Ray Kroc was always looking for the ultimate product he could peddle.

In fact, it was Multimixers that first drew Kroc to the McDonald brothers' hamburger stand. After all, if he could discover the secret of how they sold 20,000 shakes each month, how many more milkshake machines could he sell? But when Kroc showed up at McDonald's shortly before noon one morning in 1954 and saw the rapidly moving line of customers buying bags of burgers and fries, he had but one thought: "This will go anyplace. Anyplace!"

After the McDonald brothers explained that they had neither the energy nor the desire to oversee a nationwide expansion, Kroc convinced them to sign him on as their exclusive franchising agent for the entire country. He formed the new franchising company on March 2, 1955 under the name of McDonald's System, Inc. and opened his prototype McDonald's restaurant in Des Plaines, Illinois on April 15, 1955. It now serves as an official company museum.

As it turned out, a great salesman had finally discovered his ultimate product.

Rather than tinker with a successful format, Kroc not only retained the McDonald's name, but he also kept the McDonald's formula of a limited menu, quality food, an assembly-line production system, and fast, friendly service. He added his own demanding standards for cleanliness, creating McDonald's mantra of QSC (Quality, Service, and Cleanliness)—a formula for running a successful restaurant that continues as McDonald's operating principle today, along with the addition of "V" for Value.

It was in the area of franchising and supply where Kroc uniquely applied the lessons of his sales background to create a successful organization. In many ways, it was a matter of necessity, but Kroc also knew from his experience that there were always many good ideas throughout an organization and, by creating interdependence among its people, innovation would blossom.

Kroc's agreement with the McDonald brothers was to limit the franchise fee to $950 per restaurant and charge a service fee of 1.9 percent of restaurant sales—with 0.5 percent of the proceeds going back to the McDonald brothers. That was a very slim margin, so it was in Kroc's best interest to do everything possible to ensure that his franchise owners could build their sales. If they failed, he would fail with them.

In addition, Kroc decided that the McDonald's system would not be in the business of selling its franchise owners anything—not their equipment, supplies, food, or packaging. Kroc had seen too many franchise systems make their franchisees purchase expensive equipment and supplies from the company as a condition of doing business—ensuring the short-term success of the franchisor, but putting the franchisees at a long-time competitive disadvantage.

So Kroc signed up independent suppliers—on the basis of a handshake—based upon the quality of their products and their ability to deliver value to the restaurants. Loyalty was the key. McDonald's did not jump from supplier to supplier on the basis of a few pennies in savings. At the same time, suppliers knew if McDonald's prospered the volume of their own business would grow.

Finally, the company purchased or leased much of the real estate the restaurants were located upon, a program that soon produced a valuable competitive asset in its own right.

Three-Legged Stool

Thus, the three legs of the McDonald's stool were created—the franchisees, the suppliers, and the company. Like a three-legged stool, each leg had to be equally strong to support the business. While such a partnering alliance is still unusual today, it was virtually unheard of in the mid-1950s.

And the three-legged stool has proven itself many times over, providing McDonald's with a competitive advantage within the growing quick-service restaurant industry.

That was the context in which Ray Kroc used to say, "None of us is as good as all of us." But, as the years went by and as the make-up of the company's personnel became more complex, its meaning within McDonald's expanded to include our approach to diversity development. But first things first—McDonald's had to survive its infancy.

At the end of 1956, its first full year of operations, McDonald's had a total of 14 restaurants. Sales for the year totaled $1.2 million. Bender, who had helped Kroc open his own Des Plaines restaurant, became his first official franchisee when he opened a restaurant in Fresno, California. Several of the initial franchisees who followed Bender were Kroc's golfing buddies at the Rolling Green Country Club in Arlington Heights, Illinois.

Four years later, as word about this new franchising opportunity began to spread, McDonald's had 228 restaurants reporting $37.6 million in sales. However, Kroc was finding his agreement with the McDonald brothers too restrictive and he wasn't able to generate enough capital to expand and meet demand. The company's profit was just $77,000 in 1960 and Kroc's new firm was already carrying $5.7 million in long-term debt.

So Kroc offered to buy the brothers out of the business in order to gain the flexibility he needed to grow rapidly and still maintain tight controls over the operating standards at each of the restaurants. The two McDonald brothers asked for a flat $2.7 million in cash—a fair price at the time for inventing the fast-food industry, they thought. They would pay $700,000 in taxes, and then be able to retire as millionaires with an even $1 million each. (That's the equivalent of more than $6.7 million in today's dollars, although it should be noted that, if the brothers still earned one-half of one percent of McDonald's sales, their estates' share would have amounted to more than *$318 million* in 2008 alone.)

Kroc was already strapped for cash, but he managed to obtain a loan based on the company's real estate values and meet the brothers' terms. Though it ultimately cost him $14 million to repay it over a five and a half year period, Kroc had purchased the ability to control the fate of his growing system.

Hamburger University Is Born

That same year, Fred Turner, who had started as a grillman in Kroc's first restaurant in 1956 and risen to become Kroc's right-hand operations chief, opened Hamburger University in the basement of a restaurant in Elk Grove Village, Illinois. This was McDonald's first training facility for new franchisees and store managers, and it has since grown into a worldwide institution featuring sophisticated training techniques, high-level management courses, and, of course, a diversity training curriculum.

By the time McDonald's turned 10 years old in 1965, it had a great deal to celebrate. But, with the advantage of hindsight, it's easy to see that this rapidly growing young company had a great deal of wrenching change ahead of it as it was pressured by the same forces that were to prove so disruptive in society in general.

McDonald's had grown to 738 restaurants by the end of 1965, each of them staffed exclusively with men. As the *McDonald's Manual*, first published by Fred Turner in 1958, clearly stated at the time: "McDonald's units employ only male employees, unless permission is obtained from McDonald's System, Inc. Otherwise, the only exception is the wife or daughter of the owner. Then in such cases a white uniform is to be worn."

The manual described a restaurant's personnel as follows—the French Fry Man, the Counterman, the Grillman, the Window Man, the Milk Shake Man, and the Maintenance Man. Staffing a restaurant exclusively with men began when the McDonald brothers eliminated their drive-thru operations and the roller-skating girls who would take orders from the parked cars. Ray Kroc saw a male-only restaurant staff as a way to foster a family atmosphere in the restaurants without the distraction of staff members flirting with each other. The Window Man in particular was a key to running a successful restaurant, according to the *Operations Manual*:

> It is advisable to choose employees for the window operation
> who make a good appearance, have an immediately likeable
> personality, are fast with their movements, and are above
> average in intelligence. Their hats, shirts, and aprons should
> never be in a soiled state. In the summertime, a band of sweat
> will be noticeable around the front of the cap. These caps
> should be worn down over the hairline with the emblem "I'm
> Speedee" forward. Window men must begin each day wearing

a fresh shirt and apron. A clean cut individual who keeps his hair trimmed, pants pressed, fingernails clean, and shoes polished will make the best appearance.

As you can see, this was clearly a "men's only" manual, but this excerpt also provides a good insight into the meticulous detail that went into running a successful restaurant.

A Pivotal Year

The company's tenth year was pivotal in a number of ways. McDonald's made its first public stock offering in 1965 at $22.50 per share, ran its first national commercial that introduced Ronald McDonald as part of its sponsorship of the Macy's Parade, and held its first convention for owner/operators in Hollywood, Florida.

In fact, the initial announcement for the Convention inadvertently showed the thinking of the time when it said, "The purpose of this meeting is the discussion of subjects in relation to unit operation and management. This meeting will also afford you the opportunity to exchange ideas and experiences with fellow McDonald's operators, while the wives are playing cards or relaxing at the pool."

Interestingly, despite these obvious signs of the times that seem almost funny to look back upon today, there was one woman who played an extremely significant role in the early success of the company—June Martino, Ray Kroc's secretary. I never knew Martino personally, but she was described by people who worked with her as enterprising, direct, aggressive, convivial, and slightly offbeat.

Martino had been Ray Kroc's secretary and bookkeeper when he was still selling Multimixers, and, while she continued as his secretary at McDonald's, she also played a much larger role in the development of the company.

For one thing, Martino was instrumental in steering many people toward jobs at McDonald's in the early days. In fact, one of

Martino's recruits was a college student hired to work in the mailroom named Mike Quinlan, who was later my boss for a while and then went on to serve as McDonald's chairman and CEO.

The Peace Maker

A second key role that Martino played was maintaining balance in a pressurized environment where several different, strong personalities were clashing with each other over the best way to make McDonald's successful.

Martino was the mediator in the center of everything, including a long-standing feud between Kroc and Harry Sonneborn, the company's first CEO, as the two men sometimes went months without talking directly to each other. As Fred Turner later put it: "June was the glue."

As Turner recalled at a Women's Leadership Network conference in 2007, Kroc and Sonneborn were opposites—they didn't really get along and didn't care very much for each other. "If they were disagreeing on something that was holding up progress, June Martino would go in, sit down with one, and talk to him," Turner said. "Then she'd leave, go off to the other, and come back with an answer. She would finesse it, and I don't think she always told the other guy the whole truth. It might sound chauvinistic to call her the housemother, but in my world, the housemother was in charge. You didn't cross her back in those days. June was incredible."

Martino played such a critically important role in shaping the McDonald's organization and holding it together in the early years that she was awarded 10 percent equity in the small company because Kroc felt he couldn't pay her what she was really worth. She was ultimately named Corporate Secretary and Treasurer, and a member of the Board of Directors. When McDonald's took its stock public in 1965, Martino, a mother of 10 children (8 of them adopted), not only became worth $5 million (or some $31 million in today's value), but she also became the first woman since Queen Elizabeth to dine in the all-male dining room of the New York Stock Exchange.

I have always felt that the unique role that June Martino played in the early days of McDonald's was a preview of the open mind toward diversity that was to come in the future as the company grew and matured.

First, though, there was a rude awakening in store for McDonald's, and everybody else in the corporate world.

Lessons Learned

The seeds that can blossom into diversity are often planted long before you realize it.

In our early years, McDonald's did not feature diversity as we know it today within our ranks—in fact, the idea of diversity was an alien concept to anyone in the company, and to society in general at that time in history. But the qualities that later led McDonald's to flourish and embrace diversity in subsequent years did exist in those early days—and those were our core values.

I would suggest that every company has values that you can build upon to create a successful diversity initiative—whether you are starting from scratch or working to improve earlier efforts. You just have to look for them and apply them to your current circumstance.

For example, McDonald's belief in the value of the three-legged stool among our franchisees, our suppliers, and our employees represented a commitment to the need for everyone within our system to do well in order for the system to do well. That value translated well as we began to diversify in later years because we believed that everyone needed to contribute to, and profit from, active participation in the system. Our networking to support our business in the early days prompted networking to support our diversity groups later on.

Similarly, our emphasis on the value of training and education in running great restaurants was a foundation for our later efforts in making our diversity efforts successful. We used those same training and education tools to not only enhance the ability for people to prosper within McDonald's, but also to help our existing leaders understand how to manage diversity to advance the company's business goals.

The lesson I would share from this experience is that you can look back into the history of your own organization to determine your unique core values and use these qualities as foundational building blocks for your own diversity efforts.

When you build upon fundamental beliefs like fairness, honesty, integrity, and opportunity, you give your own people a common ground of understanding about the value of diversity and inclusion. That way, you can tap into the founding experience of your organization to enhance your own efforts to increase the effectiveness of your initiatives to build a diverse workforce.

3

Awakening

From all accounts, Ray Kroc's small but growing hamburger company was a reflection of his own personality and probably fairly typical for companies in the post-World War II era. Kroc was proud of his immigrant heritage and he firmly believed that anyone in America could succeed through hard work and dedication, just like he did. And even though his management team at McDonald's—with the exception of June Martino—consisted of all white males, they did reflect a diverse collection of ethnic, religious, and educational backgrounds.

Roland Jones was the first African American employee to work as a field consultant for the corporation, which meant that he oversaw and advised a number of franchisees on the operations of their restaurants. Jones recalls that Kroc was opinionated about many subjects and had some eccentric views, but none of them had to do with race. "He was often naïve and could be less than sensitive to the broad social issues of racism, sexism, and other forms of prejudice," Jones writes in his book, *Standing Up & Standing Out.* "I don't think that Mr. Kroc and most of the corporate executives at McDonald's back then could ever fully grasp the depth and breadth of the cultural and economic disparity between white male Americans and the rest of us. . . . He loved McDonald's and all the people who were part of it. Whatever position a person held in the company, Mr. Kroc expected him or her to work hard, perform with competence, put the customer first, and most important, be loyal to McDonald's mission and standards—just what he expected of himself."

Even Ray Kroc's ban on women working in the restaurants came out of his desire for McDonald's to be a family friendly place to eat. Several people told me that it had its roots after World War II, when every guy who had been a mess chef came out of the Army and started a restaurant. They had a reputation of having a toothpick in their mouths, a pack of cigarettes rolled up in their sleeves, and a penchant for making advances on all the waitresses in the restaurants.

Ray wanted to avoid this kind of "hanky panky" and so he followed the lead of Dick and Mac McDonald, who had done away with female carhops in their drive-in days because the teen-aged boys they attracted to the restaurant tended to crowd out the family trade.

Practical Reasons

This practice was discontinued for very practical reasons in the mid-1960s—we couldn't find enough employees to staff our rapidly growing chain of restaurants, especially when so many young men were being drafted to fight the war in Vietnam. The first exception allowing women to work in a restaurant came when the company hired "Day Ladies"—mothers who would come in to staff the restaurants during school hours. But the real impetus for change came from the franchisees, who hired young women out of necessity.

Ed Rensi, who later rose to become president of McDonald's USA, recalls the company sending him to Springfield, Ohio as a young field consultant to stop an owner/operator who was discovered to be hiring women. "I was told in no uncertain terms that it was none of my business who he hired, and I was sent back home," Rensi says with a laugh. "So I don't think there was a conscious decision in the late 1960s that we're going to start doing the right thing now by hiring women in the restaurants; it just started to happen."

It took more dramatic events to change the company's approach in the matter of race.

While the Civil Rights movement had been making progress for some time following the U.S. Supreme Court's landmark Brown v. Board of Education ruling in 1954, for most Americans the struggle appeared to be primarily a "Southern state" phenomenon until the late 1960s.

Rosa Parks took her historic bus ride in Montgomery, Alabama in 1955, leading to a year-long boycott; Arkansas Governor Orvil Faubus blocked nine black high school students from entering a formerly all-white school in 1957, forcing President Eisenhower to send in federal troops; violence and riots that broke out when James Meredith became the first black student to enroll at the University of Mississippi in 1961 forced President Kennedy to send in federal troops; and black marchers for voting rights were brutalized in Montgomery, Alabama in 1965.

But it wasn't until race riots outside the South in the mid- to late-1960s and the assassination of Dr. Martin Luther King, Jr. occurred that the Civil Rights movement gained true prominence across all of America. There were riots in the Watts area of Los Angeles in 1965 and in Newark and Detroit in the summer of 1967, and then Dr. King's death in April of 1967. Suddenly, for the first time, companies who were seeking to do business with a variety of people from all over the country found that there were significant challenges in the inner cities and some monumental inequities to overcome. This was a different world, and it would take a different approach to overcome these barriers.

Franchisee on Leading Edge

Once again, McDonald's owner/operators were on the forefront in pointing the way to the future—in this case, it was two men who co-owned the franchise in Washington, D.C. who opened the door the widest.

In 1956, John Gibson and Oscar Goldstein had made a deal with Kroc for the exclusive franchise of the metropolitan Washington area. The territory included the District of Columbia, five counties in Virginia, and three counties in Maryland. Gibson was a beer distributor and Goldstein was the owner of a tavern and delicatessen that was one of Gibson's customers. Their company—known as Gee Gee Corporation—had become one of the company's early franchising success stories.

For one thing, they were responsible for creating Ronald McDonald, who went on to become the best-known clown in the world. The original Ronald was played by Willard Scott, who later became the weatherman on NBC's Today Show. Using Ronald McDonald as a television pitchman was so successful at generating sales that, at one point, the Gee Gee organization was spending more money on advertising than even McDonald's Corporation itself.

Ultimately, Gee Gee grew into a franchise with 43 restaurants before McDonald's bought it back for a total of $16.8 million in 1967. But, because of Washington, D.C.'s racial mix, the Gee Gee organization had another asset that proved just as valuable as Ronald McDonald, if not as immediately visible—experienced African American managers.

Gee Gee had hired large numbers of black employees to staff their restaurants—again, a move born out of necessity. And, in the process, many had moved up through the organization to become restaurant managers, area supervisors who oversaw several restaurants at a time, and field consultants. Indeed, in the violence that followed Martin Luther King's assassination, it was only safe for African American store managers to go into many areas of the city to operate its restaurants, so Carl Osborne, a black manager who had been supervising five stores, was given responsibility for operations in all 12 inner-city restaurants.

After buying back the franchise, McDonald's mined Gee Gee's employee ranks to staff its own corporate cadre of African

American leaders, including Osborne, Roland Jones, Bob Beavers, Cosmo Williams, John French, Joe Brown, and many others. But it took some pioneers to go first . . . and that began with Herman Petty, who became McDonald's first African American franchisee in 1968.

African American Entrepreneurs

One of the major challenges in recruiting minority franchisees to own and operate McDonald's restaurants, especially in the inner cities, was the cost of investing in a restaurant. In the late 1960s, franchisee candidates were expected to invest an average of about $150,000 for a turnkey restaurant—an amount that was way over the head of most prospective minority owner/operators.

The original attempt to solve this problem was to find white investors who would financially support black franchisees who were interested in running inner-city restaurants. These arrangements stretched the company's traditional rules that the person investing in the restaurant must also operate the restaurant. They were called "salt and pepper," or "zebra," partnerships.

Herman Petty was originally approached to run a restaurant by two white investors in the Chicago area—Arthur DuPlessic and Joseph Greenberg. They encouraged Petty to go out to McDonald's, where he put in an application and interviewed with Ed Schmitt, the Chicago Regional Manager at the time. I later worked for Ed myself after he became president of McDonald's Corporation, and I know from first-hand knowledge that he was very interested in bringing African Americans into our franchising family.

Petty was a native of Chicago's South Side, had served in the military, and graduated from Chicago's Roosevelt University, my own alma mater. Petty ran a barbershop, just like his father before him, and he also worked for the Chicago Transit Authority at night. That barbershop in Chicago's Stoney Island neighborhood turned out to be just a few blocks from where his first restaurant was located—indeed, it was just the eighth store that had been opened by one of Kroc's first franchisees back in June of 1956.

Like so many McDonald's decisions, when they called Petty back to tell him he was accepted, he had to act fast. They called him at nine o'clock on a Monday morning and asked him to start his Hamburger University training at one o'clock that afternoon. He arranged to get his in-store training at a restaurant adjacent to the HU facility in Elk Grove, going to that restaurant as soon as the formal classes were over. And then they awarded him, and his silent partners, his first restaurant.

Gang Territory

Business at the restaurant was not doing well when Petty took over, primarily because it was in the heart of the Blackstone Rangers' youth gang territory, and removing them as employees, and loiterers in the store, became his first priority.

"Because I had a barbershop down the street, I knew everybody in the neighborhood and they knew me," Petty recalls. "I knew these kids and I knew their families, and I was able to get them all out of the store. At that time, McDonald's didn't have women working in the stores, but I hired women, all grown women.

"After I got those ladies trained, I went to the military recruiting office and hired guys who came out of the service so they would become managers and trainers in my system. The military is like McDonald's—they produce young men who are oriented, sharp, clean, and know how to take orders, and know how to give orders."

Concurrently with making Herman Petty McDonald's first black franchisee, the company brought in Roland Jones from Washington, D.C. and promoted him to become our first black field consultant. He was assigned several restaurants in the Chicago region, including Petty's. Jones spent a great deal of time with Petty, who had never operated a restaurant before. Because the physical facility was run down and the equipment mostly broken, it was hard to set priorities because everything was a priority, according to Jones.

Initial Success

Thanks to their tireless efforts, Herman Petty and Roland Jones made that first black-owned McDonald's a success, increasing sales by some 75 percent in the first year. Petty took over a second store in 1969, and Jones began adding additional black-owned inner-city restaurants to his list of consulting clients.

The original "salt and pepper" financing arrangements turned out to be a disaster, however. The silent partners were found to have quietly included high "management fees" as part of their compensation, neglected reinvestments in the restaurants and equipment, failed to pay many vendors and suppliers, and ultimately began racing each other to clean cash out of the registers each day.

It took a full year for Burt Cohen, our head of franchising at the time, to untangle the arrangements at a cost of $500,000 to McDonald's, but when he was finished, there were eight new black owner/operators owning and controlling their own restaurants and the two white investors had been forced out.

More important, McDonald's had awakened to the challenge ahead of us and we had begun the long journey of diversifying our business, both inside and out. Like everything we did in our business, the only way we knew to operate was at full speed ahead.

Lessons Learned

An essential ingredient in leading the growth of a successful enterprise is the ability to identify and anticipate change.

Every business leader knows that changing trends in the market-place will require their organization to innovate and develop new products and services to meet the shifting desires of consumers. There's no debate about this—you either keep pace with change or you wither and die.

But, as we have seen in this chapter, there are even bigger issues of change that can affect an entire society, and organizations within that society also need to adapt and change internal attitudes and behaviors in response to these larger movements.

The lesson that McDonald's learned during the tumultuous times of the 1960s, for example, was both simple and profound: We needed to change the complexion of our company to survive in a society that was dramatically changing all around us. If we were to continue to grow and expand, we needed to recognize the new realities of the world in which we operated and change our approach.

In our case, deciding to change was the easy part. The process itself was difficult; it entailed a lot of trial and error because we were on uncharted ground, and many people in the organization had to confront, and change, long-standing attitudes and beliefs.

The key ingredient in staying the course was management commitment—a determination by our top managers, starting with Ray Kroc and Fred Turner, that we needed to be a diverse organization to compete in a changing society. They provided what many in our organization called "air cover," the quiet backing and support that people needed as they worked to find ways to increase our diversity.

That's why I would say to anyone today that management commitment is a key ingredient to changing your own organization. It has to come from the top.

As you look at society today in the United States, there is no question that we have embraced diversity to a greater degree than ever before—at all levels. As a result, the organizations that have not learned how to manage diversity within their own workforce will continue to be at a distinct competitive disadvantage against others that have . . . and the gap will only widen in the future.

So, if you find yourself lagging behind your competitors in the area of diversity, it is imperative that you recognize that you are not in step with current trends in society and that you need to change.

As we learned many years ago at McDonald's, it is impossible to make meaningful change within any organization without a clear and compelling commitment from the leaders at the very top levels.

4

The
African American
Experience

*B*ob Beavers was one of the many African American employees brought into McDonald's home office from Washington, D.C. to help diversify the owner/operator base. In the course of his own career, he rose through the ranks to serve on McDonald's Board of Directors for 27 years. Like so many McDonald's employees, he started working in a restaurant not thinking that he would find a career under the Golden Arches.

"I was a junior in college in 1963 and had taken a government examination to work part time, but my girlfriend said there was a sign in the window of a McDonald's just a few blocks from my house, so I went in and applied and two days later I was working there," Beavers recalls.

"Most of my colleagues had a similar experience, although many of them went into management training at first while I started out cleaning trash cans and washing windows at a buck an hour and worked my way up."

In 1969, Fred Turner, Ray Kroc's right-hand man in running the company, brought Beavers into the corporate licensing office to help find talented African American franchisees for the system. "When I was being interviewed, I got the tour of our offices, which covered three floors of the building on LaSalle Street," Beavers remembers. "There was not a single person of color in the entire building, which was not a comforting feeling. I didn't see anybody like me, not even a secretary, not even a clerk, male or female."

Management Support

At that point, McDonald's had grown to some 1,300 restaurants and was looking to step up the pace of its expansion. According to Beavers, Turner had plans to increase McDonald's new restaurant openings to two or three hundred each year, and he could see that we were not going to develop McDonald's in neighborhoods across the country unless we had good representation with African American and Hispanic franchisees.

In recalling his initial interview with Turner, Beavers sums up the environment of the time by saying, "For the most part, management at McDonald's was very supportive of the fact that they were acting to integrate the system, both from the employee standpoint and the franchisee community. Fred knew that there were going to be problems and issues and that there was going to be a lot of prejudice out there and a lot of push-back, but he wanted it to happen."

Most people I talked with remember Turner as preferring to stay in the background, but they could detect his influence on events behind the scenes from time to time. As a matter of fact, when Beavers first visited the Los Angeles regional office, he was confronted by a local construction manager for the company who demanded to know what right he had to come into a McDonald's office. Word of the confrontation managed to get back to Turner. The construction manager left the company a couple of weeks later.

This very first effort to diversify McDonald's clearly had management support from the very top of the organization, even though it was not always completely visible.

Bringing in Franchisees

Beavers initially put together what he called a 50-2 program to bring in 50 minority franchisees over a two-year period. After two years, he had actually exceeded that ambitious goal. One of the key factors that helped potential African American franchisees overcome the investment hurdles to restaurant ownership was a new understanding with the Small Business Administration and its SBA loan guarantee program.

As Beavers recalls, many franchisee candidates could put together $30,000 to $40,000 out of their life savings, but that wasn't enough to buy into their first restaurant. However, they could make up the difference with an SBA 90 percent guaranteed loan, which meant that the most that a lender would be out of pocket if the loan failed was 10 percent. The problem was that the bureaucratic red tape was such that the loan guarantees could not be issued in a timely fashion for the quick, on-the-spot, act-now decisions that characterized McDonald's way of doing business.

Beavers met with Art McZier, who was the SBA deputy administrator and the first black person to hold a key position within the SBA administration, and explained the problem. McZier then went to McDonald's downtown Chicago office and met with Turner privately for an hour. When McZier emerged from the office, Beavers could tell from the look on his face that McZier "got it."

Shortly after that, a letter went out to all SBA offices saying that McDonald's was being very aggressive in bringing minorities into the system and that the SBA was going to step up and do whatever possible to help us do that. All of a sudden, the pace of bringing in black franchisees stepped up noticeably.

Meanwhile, the rapidly growing African American franchisee base was creating new challenges for field consultants like Roland Jones, who had spent so much time and effort bringing Herman Petty up to speed in all the operational details of running a McDonald's restaurant. Now, his cascload of new inner-city African American franchisees was expanding rapidly, and there were not enough hours in the day for him to devote the same amount of attention to each of the new owner/operators as he had given to Petty.

According to Jones, Petty asked a prophetic question: Why don't you get us together and train us as a group?

Our First Network

And that's exactly what they did, providing the origins of the networking concept that continues within McDonald's to this day. It started with a series of weekly meetings with Chicago franchisees in the back room of a local tavern—meetings that included Jones and Mike Quinlan, a young district manager who would ultimately rise to become Turner's successor as McDonald's CEO.

With Quinlan's backing, they began to bring instructors and classes into Chicago, renting different halls and hotel meeting rooms for the training sessions for franchisees and their store managers. Ultimately, the company bought a building on the South Side of Chicago that it converted into its meeting hall and classroom.

The local networking effort soon extended to new African American franchisees from around the country who flew into Chicago on Ray Kroc's company plane to take advantage of the focused training opportunity. As Petty recalls, "All new black operators would come in to Chicago and we would help to train them. Then we would take our managers and crews and stay with them for their first two weeks in their new restaurant to get them going. Kroc gave us the corporate airplane and a company bus to do all these things."

So, in addition to top management support, McDonald's found a way to customize and streamline its training program to help its new African American franchisees get their restaurants up and running.

Trouble in Cleveland

It didn't take long for McDonald's inner-city strategy to be tested under fire in the City of Cleveland, where two of the restaurants franchised by Orville Benson in a rapidly changing neighborhood started being picketed by residents in 1968.

"The local management team just didn't get it and they were very insulting to customers," Beavers recalls. "So the people went down the street to a community organizer—David Hill, who called himself 'Rabbi Hill,' although I don't think he was a rabbi—and they began picketing the restaurants."

The first thing Beavers did was sit down with the owner/operator and let him know that he would have to sell his restaurants. It wasn't just because he would never make any money with them, but they were also drawing adverse publicity for the entire McDonald's system. Indeed, there was already talk of a citywide boycott of McDonald's in Cleveland.

Several other African American members of the Gee Gee organization in Washington, D.C. came into the two embattled stores in Cleveland to keep them operating as Beavers set out to find a viable prospect to take over the franchise. He ultimately recruited Chuck Johnson, a former U.S. marshal who was a good friend of Carl Stokes, the mayor of Cleveland. Johnson was quickly approved and trained, and then he purchased the franchise.

But the community groups refused to believe that Johnson was anything but a "front" for the company, and they backed up their demands to find their own franchisees with intimidating tactics, like brandishing walking sticks and sending anonymous death threats.

"Finally, after about a year, we were able to start getting traffic back into the restaurants," Beavers says. "But Rabbi Hill and his people were collecting money from unsuspecting folks by promising to get them a franchise. One woman gave him over thirty thousand dollars and she never saw the money again."

McDonald's would never agree to allow outside groups to select its franchisees.

"Shoot to Kill"

Tensions were running so high at the height of the boycott that Beavers would have to register at his Cleveland hotel under an assumed name. At one point, a policeman gave him a gun for self-protection, telling Beavers, "If you have to use it, shoot to kill!"

The turning point came when Dr. Kenneth Clement, a prominent African American who helped Mayor Stokes get elected, called the boycott a "shakedown" in an article written in the Cleveland

Call and Post. The boycott ended, we found our own black franchisees for six Cleveland restaurants, and Rabbi Hill fled to Guyana after being convicted of blackmail in association with his scheme to sell McDonald's franchises.

Interestingly, it took some time for the message learned in Cleveland to filter throughout the system. Ed Rensi was a field consultant in our Cleveland region at the time and remembers a field service meeting in Chicago where every region was supposed to make a presentation on a topic other than field service.

"We decided to talk about our experiences in the African American world in Cleveland and what was involved in dealing with the issues and doing it the right way by training and embracing people," Rensi says. "We were told by the then-national field service manager that we weren't allowed to talk or present on that subject and we basically told them that, if we couldn't do that, we were packing up our bags and going home."

But the story wasn't over as far as education went. After the first day at the meeting, Rensi and a couple of other white McDonald's executives were joined in their room at the Holiday Inn in Elk Grove, Illinois by African Americans Roland Jones and Joe Brown. "They proceeded to teach us what it was like to be black in America and, more particularly, what it was like to be black in McDonald's," Rensi recalls. "That was probably the most intense dialogue I've ever had in my life, and at that point I fell in love with Brown and Jones because they were incredibly honest men."

Sending a Message

Nonetheless, by one means or another, the Cleveland experience began to send a clear message throughout the McDonald's system: A proactive approach to minority licensing was the only way to avoid similar situations in major cities across the country. And as the numbers of African American owner/operators began to increase, the need for networking—the third plank of diversity along with management support and training—increased as well. Like most everything that takes place at McDonald's, it began with the restaurants and the increasing number of African Americans who were becoming owner/operators of those restaurants.

With the training effort centered in Chicago, which was also the initial focal point of the company's minority recruiting efforts, it's only natural that the Black McDonald's Operators Association (BMOA) was born in Chicago as well.

Herman Petty recalls that it began simply as a weekly meeting of African American owner/operators. "We met the first time when we got the classes started in the classrooms, and then we moved to a nightclub where we met in a lounge in the back," Petty says. "Mike Quinlan, our white district manager, led our meeting every Monday night with us, and he, Roland, and four of us operators put the BMOA together. We were not a militant group. We wanted to prove to McDonald's that we could be as good as the other operators, and we wanted to prove to the community that we could be as good, so the training went on and we worked on."

In formalizing the group in 1970, the initial handful of members elected Ed Wimp, who was already operating four inner-city restaurants, as its President. Primarily a Chicago group focused around training and self-help, the initial BMOA members held a meeting for all black operators who attended the company's International Convention in Hawaii in 1971.

The first convention held by the Chicago BMOA in 1972 was a small, two-day affair aimed at improving communications among the black operators in the system and the company, but once again the Midwest region—including Detroit, Cleveland, Toledo, Dayton, and Columbus—did not send any franchisees or employees. Jones, who organized the meeting, explains it this way: "As long as the BMOA was localized to the Midwest, confined to one field consultant, and focused on training and self-improvement, it had been accepted as a positive by the executives. . . . But the prospect of black operators unifying across regional lines would have raised a red flag."

Sowing the Seeds

However, that first meeting, presided over by Petty, sowed the seeds for the formation of the National Black McDonald's Operators Association (NBMOA). The organization adopted the structure that it still operates under to this day at a Philadelphia convention in 1976, where Ralph Kelly, an owner/operator from Detroit, was elected the first NBMOA president. Carl Osborne, Sr., who had started his career in the Gee Gee organization and who had been the first African American restaurant supervisor before becoming an owner/operator, served as the second president in 1978. Jones himself, who had left the company to become a franchisee in Nashville, was the third NBMOA president, elected to his two-year term in 1980.

Emerging as it did in the midst of rapid, and sometimes even chaotic, growth for McDonald's as a whole, the NBMOA's growing list of members represented a powerful self-help group of franchisees who had a unique view of operating restaurants in the inner cities. From 1968 through 1978, for example, the McDonald's system grew from 1,087 to 5,185 restaurants and from 3 countries to 25. And the NBMOA's influence was felt far beyond just its own restaurants.

Voice of the Customers

The NBMOA lobbied for the creation of advertising and marketing aimed at African American consumers, and that's how Tom Burrell and his new advertising agency in Chicago became affiliated with McDonald's—a relationship that continues to this day.

Burrell, who started his career in the mailroom of Wade Advertising in Chicago, opened his own firm in 1971 with the aim of creating effective advertising for African Americans. It was located in a small office on North Michigan Avenue in Chicago, across the hall from McDonald's public relations firm of GolinHarris.

Roland Jones brought Burrell to the 1973 BMOA convention, where he outlined his ideas for advertising to black consumers to increase sales for black owners in black communities—a very new concept at the time. Jones recalls in his book, "Faced with the facts—the size of the African American market and its collective purchasing power—McDonald's got the message years before many other large corporations. It was shortly after the BMOA convention that McDonald's established a direct reporting relationship with Burrell Advertising."

Thanks to his early and ongoing success with McDonald's, Burrell began directing minority marketing campaigns for many other large corporate clients, including Coca-Cola, Ford, and Procter & Gamble.

Pattern for Success

As the number of NBMOA operators increased, they not only made the need for increased numbers of African American employees within McDonald's abundantly clear, but they also began to create a pipeline of their own restaurant employees who were ready for promotion to the corporation. In time, they also created opportunities for increased black employment within McDonald's corps of suppliers. And, as I'll discuss later, they spurred the development of black-owned suppliers for the system.

So the pattern for success in integrating McDonald's franchisees—management support, training, and networking—became the framework that was used to promote diversity within McDonald's own employee ranks. Once again, it was not a clear and simple path.

The employee support started with the creation of a Fast Track program, called Accelerated Management Development, in which McDonald's would recruit and hire promising African American prospects and advance them through the ranks. One of the earliest hires was a young man named Reggie Webb, who would go on to have a profound influence on the company throughout his career.

Webb was a native of South Bend, Indiana, who graduated from California State University in Los Angeles with a degree in political science and went to work in a Los Angeles Community Action Agency that was part of the early War on Poverty. As his friends began moving into private sector jobs, he became aware of McDonald's Fast Track program and joined the company in 1973 in operations training.

Webb became the company's second African American field consultant and, like Roland Jones before him, was assigned to help three new black franchisees in the Los Angeles area who had also been brought in with those original "salt and pepper" silent partners, DuPlessie and Greenberg. Webb moved through the local ranks with alacrity, serving as a field consultant, area restaurant supervisor, sales manager, director of McOpCo (McDonald's company-owned restaurants), director of operations, and then to the home office in Oak Brook, Illinois as a director in the National Operations department in 1978.

"A number of people felt that opportunity was limited by discriminatory practices, but I found my experience to be more the standard for a corporation, where you are promoted if you perform well," Webb recalls. "To many, it was obvious to see the value to the enterprise that would come from enhancing the role of our African American employees, but frankly, we didn't know exactly what to do. We were a microcosm of the America of the day—no worse, and maybe some better."

Webb remembers that Fred Turner and Ed Schmitt were very supportive of the effort to bring in African American employees back then, and Ed Rensi was similarly motivated later on. "Each had their own inimitable way and each understood what they could do and could not do," Webb says. "They could not change the hearts of people nor the behavior of people with critical success to the enterprise."

The Birth of Training

Senior management's discussions about how to proceed took on a very practical business nature, according to Webb. The company had so many issues on its plate in the process of building the business that it wasn't productive to spend so much of its time in trying to keep people happy and resolving lawsuits.

It was clear that we needed to develop a better way.

One of the solutions was to begin an intensive training program called the Black Career Development (BCD) seminar. And that's when McDonald's began a relationship with Dr. Ron Brown, a consultant who has been advising McDonald's on diversity issues and strategies now for almost three decades.

Brown earned his doctoral degree in counseling psychology from the University of California, Berkeley and formed a firm with two other partners to advise companies on affirmative action strategies. He already had experience with major companies like Procter and Gamble, DuPont, and Philip Morris, and Webb brought him into McDonald's after a couple of employees were impressed by one of his public presentations.

However, the corporate culture Brown discovered at McDonald's when he first came into the company in 1979 was unlike anything he had seen before.

"When I hit McDonald's, we're talking about wild and crazy guys," Brown recalls. "The whole tone, the whole energy, was different. The company was making a lot of money and these guys were spending it and there was a sense that they could do anything they wanted to do.

"And, in a sense, that's what part of the problem was for African American employees. This was such a free form, undisciplined organization that blacks could not figure out how they could succeed here. There was order in it once you got past the wild and crazy individualism, but it was just the style in which these guys ran it. So we started talking about building individual power, because that's what you needed here."

As Webb remembers it, one of the most eye-opening aspects of BCD for minority employees was the realization that the way McDonald's operated was not based on discriminatory practices or prejudicial attitudes.

"In many cases, the problems we had with people were not of a racial nature; they were of a corporation's cultural nature," Webb says. "African Americans looked at certain practices as things that they had to subjugate themselves to, and when they refused, that increased our turnover rate. But what they weren't understanding was that there were things that everybody had to do, and this was a cultural difference in how you take things."

Brown knew it was rare for a company to have the kind of flexibility to allow such a training program to exist inside its walls. Despite some leeriness on the part of senior management, the upside of McDonald's individualistic approach was that the company wasn't afraid to try things. And it wasn't long before the word of mouth got around throughout the company: If you're a black employee, you can't afford to miss this class.

"Rage Classes"

Annis Alston, an African American female manager who came out of the Washington, D.C. region to set a number of firsts for McDonald's, remembers the classes as an opportunity for employees to vent their rage in the early days.

Alston originally joined McDonald's as a crew member in a restaurant managed by her brother, Ben Alston, while she was studying accounting in college. "I could work flexible hours before and after school, and my brother even let me work on the restaurant's books for some practical experience," Alston recalls. "He didn't pay me anything extra for the accounting work, though."

Discovering she liked the work at McDonald's more than accounting, she worked her way up to store manager, then became the first female African American restaurant supervisor, the first such field consultant, and the first such instructor at Hamburger University.

"The thing McDonald's didn't understand in the early days was the isolation you felt and what that meant in trying to get your job done," Alston says. "They did not understand how you felt, either as an African American or a female, and you couldn't really explain it to them because they never walked in your shoes.

"When they started those classes, you came in with anger—anger because you were given fewer stores to run and other folks were getting promoted over you and you were never getting a piece of the real pie. Being in a group was our strength because we really supported each other. It was a way to help us navigate through the waters and come out sane."

Alston ultimately became McDonald's first female African American Regional Manager. She remembers being preceded by a female regional manager and an African American regional manager, neither of whom survived for very long on the job. "At my first meeting with the owner/operators, I told them that I was black and I was female, and I understood that they got rid of a black male and a white female, but that I was there to stay," she recalls. "I told them the reason I was there was to help them make money."

Good to her word, Alston excelled in that position, and today she owns and operates six restaurants of her own in central New Jersey.

Signs of Progress

"We began to see clear progress within a couple of years, especially as the Affirmative Action department began to gear up," Brown says. "We began to see more people stepping up to the Area Supervisor position and people were getting into place in corporate positions. Within the first five years, we had created a critical mass of people who understood how McDonald's works."

Once that critical mass had been established, Brown worked with his McDonald's counterparts to create a "train the trainer" program so we could develop a cadre of our own people who could teach the BCD classes, which they still do to this day.

Mike Thompson remembers BCD as the key to breaking his personal "glass ceiling." Thompson came into McDonald's Purchasing department in 1985, rose through the ranks to become a regional manager in San Francisco and then senior VP for North America Supply Chain, before buying a majority interest in Fair Oaks Farms, a McDonald's supplier.

"BCD was probably the most impactful thing that happened to me from a diversity standpoint at McDonald's," Thompson says. "It's a course that helps you understand the angers and frustrations that you have as a person of color, how those can impact you negatively in your workplace, and how to make changes in that. It's a huge 'ah-ha!' Not only did it change me, but I then had the privilege of teaching the class for several years."

Management Training

McDonald's also conducted several efforts to educate its own management to become more sensitive to diverse cultures and provide better opportunities to be successful. And it sometimes took some tough tactics to get the attention of the management participants in those training seminars.

Raymond Mines, another Fast Track African American who joined the company in 1975 as an operations trainee, remembers early training sessions run by an outside consultant named C.T. Vivian: "I called him a militant trainer," Mines says. "He used very tough tactics to get people's attention, but that's what was needed to change people's attitudes of the times. He helped make training a very important factor in advancing diversity at McDonald's."

Rensi remembers that Vivian would spend the first two days of a week-long seminar insulting and abusing the white participants and then he would finally stop and say, "Now you know how I live my life every day. Now, do you have your minds open enough that I can teach you something?" Rensi says, "People who worked for me hated my guts for bringing him in, but I'll tell you what—he made people sit up and listen."

Employee Networks

Those training seminars have been updated through the years and they continue today, although the need for such a confrontational edge has receded. In addition, we instituted the beginnings of a networking program so that black employees could help each other succeed much like the black franchisees did through the NBMOA.

It started as a Big Brother and Big Sister program—the brainchild of Cosmo Williams, another member of our African American leadership to come out of the Gee Gee organization.

Williams was born and raised in Trinidad and came to the United States to get his bachelor's degree at Howard University in Washington, D.C. After a semester in graduate school, he took time off to drive a cab to support his wife and two children and build a bankroll for the rest of his education. But when the nation's capital erupted in unrest after Dr. Martin Luther King's assassination, he discovered there were more cabs than there were tourists, so he joined McDonald's Fast Track program as an operations trainee.

Like so many others, he rose through the ranks locally and then came to the company's home office in Oak Brook, though, as he recalls, the path wasn't as easy as it sounds now. "When I first started, the attitude toward diversity was terrible," Williams says. "I had three strikes against me—I was obviously a minority, I was college educated, and I was foreign—so I had some tough times initially. But we were professional and we began to show some results for the system, and the system began to like us more and more."

When Williams arrived at the home office, he noticed the same phenomenon that Webb did—the company was hiring a lot of minorities but they were going out the back door as fast as they were coming in the front. The biggest reason was cited as "bad attitude" even though no one could ever define precisely what that meant, according to Williams.

Stop the Outflow

"We realized we had to do something to stop that vast outflow of human talent, so we decided to create what we called the Big Brother program," Williams says. "We decided to use the middle management employees in the system throughout the United States, all in the urban centers, to pull them together to help create a means by which we would save the exodus of black talent."

They launched the program with a two-day symposium in Atlanta in 1977 and it soon developed into a very effective business mentoring program. The mentors in middle management made themselves available to promising assistant restaurant managers and helped them learn how the system worked, how to overcome obstacles, and how to achieve their career goals within McDonald's.

Because the mentors used their own networks within the system to help their charges, the support, education, and encouragement began to flow, and the strong talent we were recruiting began to stay within McDonald's and advance through the company.

Affirmative Action Arrives

There was yet another important decision that management made early on, and that was to go outside the company and hire an experienced affirmative action officer—a move that had a profound influence on my career as well.

Stan Stein, at that time the head of the Personnel Department before it became Human Resources, was one of the people advocating this move, along with Reggie Webb and others. Stein had been working as a consultant to McDonald's in labor relations before he came to work for the company in 1974.

"There was no question in my mind that senior management had a sincere respect for the concept of affirmative action and diversity, but they didn't have the foggiest idea about how to accomplish it," Stein recalls. "One of the problems was that we had a bunch of white folks trying to figure it out. We needed a prominent individual in that position who brought in expertise from the outside."

As a matter of fact, the interview process turned up two excellent candidates—Mel Hopson and Rogercarole Rogers—so McDonald's hired both of them, with Mel as the head of the new department and Rogercarole as his staff director.

Hopson was born in Alabama, but his family moved to the South Side of Chicago when he was a child so his father, a laborer, and his mother, a seamstress, could provide a better life for their four children. After graduating from high school, Hopson went to Howard University, took a four-year detour in the Air Force, and then returned to Chicago to earn his degree at Roosevelt University.

Hopson took a job as an advertising copywriter at Montgomery Ward in Chicago and, after working on loan with the National Alliance of Businessmen in a minority hiring program, returned to Montgomery Ward as manager of affirmative action.

"I didn't know what affirmative action was at the time, but that was my introduction to the business and I stayed there until 1980,"

Hopson says. "When McDonald's interviewed and offered me the job, they were looking for someone who had some background and experience. I didn't want the job at first because it was part of Human Resources, and I thought it should be a special position reporting to the chairman or the president."

Direct, Combative Approach

Hopson found the McDonald's organization to be quite a bit different from the buttoned-down corporate organization at Montgomery Ward. Our company was a young, dynamic, go-get-em group of people who played hard and worked hard. And Hopson found that a direct, combative approach was the way to get things done.

"You couldn't do anything at McDonald's if you were a milquetoast guy," Hopson says. "You had to come in and tell them— you're not going to do this . . . you're going to hire X number of minorities . . . and you're going to make sure that they get developed . . . and if you don't like it, you go see the chairman and give him your complaints.

"It was important at that time to let folks know that this wasn't a game, that we were here to get things done."

Stein agrees with that assessment of the job at hand. "Mel turned out to be a very loyal employee, and he had no qualms about speaking up when that was required to fix things in the company," Stein says. "Mel's job had a lot of difficult elements. He had to deliver bad news, or report that we were not doing what we were supposed to be doing. What helped Mel is that he would take steps as long as the rationale was there, and believe me, he knew far more about the field of affirmative action than we did."

Rogers made the same observation on her early experience with the company's affirmative action program. Having interviewed with most of senior management before being hired, she knew that there was support for diversity from the top.

"However, once I got out in the field, it was crazy," Rogers says. "There wasn't a lot of understanding of what diversity was. That's what we were hired for—not necessarily to get people to love it, but to get them to understand the necessity of diversity for the company's growth and well-being."

My Career Changes Course

I had been at McDonald's for about four years when they first hired Hopson and Rogers and created the Affirmative Action department. During that time, I had been promoted from the Legal department to a job as a secretary in the executive management suite, working for Ed Schmitt, Don Smith, and then Mike Quinlan when Smith left McDonald's to work for another company.

Then I learned that a position had opened up in the Human Resources department as a compensation analyst, and I decided to try for it, since I had just about completed my undergraduate work in personnel at Roosevelt University. Ed Schmitt actually helped me get that job, having called the personnel people and saying, "Just make the right decision."

I had earned several promotions after moving to Human Resources and one of my assignments was to recruit and interview the people who staffed the Affirmative Action department from the outset. It wasn't long after that Hopson offered me a position working for him. I was reluctant at first because I really loved what I was doing, but I was encouraged to use my own professional skills, and I've been here ever since.

Do the Right Thing

I remember Hopson teaching me that affirmative action wasn't the law; it was the right thing. Equal Employment Opportunity (EEO) was the law, but McDonald's was practicing affirmative action and we were doing the positive things that would help correct some of the past wrongs.

Another distinction that was very important to McDonald's was that we were doing this on our own initiative. We didn't rely on government contracts and no one was requiring us to make this massive effort. This was something we wanted to do because it was right and because it would be good for our business, even though we knew it wouldn't be easy.

We also talked a great deal about Hopson's combative style, especially in the early days. I remember he always used to quote the Rev. Jesse Jackson: "There are tree-shakers and there are jelly-makers." Hopson saw his role as shaking the trees and doing whatever was necessary to get the fruit on the ground. He saw my role as a jelly-maker, working with others to harvest the fruit and make something good from it. And I must admit, there was a real need for some tree shaking in the beginning.

And that's where top management support came in, according to Stein. "I think through it all, Mel knew I had his back," Stein says. "Management knew that I had a high degree of respect for Mel and for his judgment because this was a guy whose neck was way out there because of me. Plus, I knew that Ed Rensi had my back."

Early Successes

We had some successes in the early days, especially within our staff functions, and none were more dramatic that in our accounting operations, where a young Jerry Calabrese was put in charge of McDonald's seven accounting centers in the field.

"The thing that made the difference was that McDonald's starting holding people accountable for diversity and began looking at the numbers," Calabrese, now vice president of Global Restaurant Measurements, recalls. "I knew that this was something that management felt was important, and you have to give them credit for being forward-looking."

Calabrese promoted Hal Reynolds, an African American on his staff, to be the head of one of the centers and he ultimately became the first department director.

"It was one of the foundational things that helped us in the accounting centers because Hal set the standards for everyone," Calabrese says. "Then we were able to recruit other people to come into our group because they could see that there was somebody like them in our senior leadership. And what gave us credibility was that no one got promoted because of color; it was all about performance."

But, while we were making progress in several of our home office operations, we found affirmative action principles to be much more difficult to implement in other parts of the country.

Challenges in the Field

One of the unique aspects of the McDonald's system is the relative autonomy of a regional manager in running the business in his or her own patch. As we continued our rapid growth throughout the country, establishing regions to manage the business was the only effective way to stay in touch with local markets, local franchisees, and local customers. But this system did have a downside, according to African American Lee Dunham, long-time owner/operator.

"In the old days, you have top management in Oak Brook and you have field consultants in the field," Dunham says. "Field consultants had 100 percent autonomy. They could do whatever they wanted to. That was the worst mistake because you cannot let one person with his prejudices, bigotry, and all of that stuff back in those days do whatever they wanted."

Our first regional office opened in California in 1964, four more were created in 1965, and, by 1980, there were 23 regional operations across the country. Ultimately, the regional operations reached a high of 40 regions in the 1990s. The regional manager made all local decisions about licensing new franchisees, granting restaurants to franchisees, hiring employees, and every other aspect of the local business. Typically, if the region's sales and profits were good, there was little if any second-guessing from the home office. That presented some challenges as Hopson went from region to region spreading the affirmative action gospel.

"We did have some racists in key positions, and by that I mean people who didn't like black people, who didn't like Hispanics or Asians, and who thought women ought to be home cooking," Hopson says. "We called them 'neanderthals', and we had to get rid of some of those people. We made sure we pointed out to the top people that a particular individual could not continue to run a region with attitudes like that if we're going to bring women and minorities in here to work."

Building Blocks

Hopson credits the existence of strong training programs and the beginnings of the employee networks upon his arrival as solid building blocks that supported our affirmative action mission. Perhaps most important was the fact that McDonald's was a consumer company and that meant that we needed to support the minority operators who were providing us an entrée to these consumer groups.

"The company found out very early on that African Americans, as an example, were the most loyal supporters of McDonald's in the marketplace," Hopson says. "But the question became, if you want to have all these customers out there, then what about your owner/operators, what about your employees, and what about your suppliers? That was the approach we took in terms of moving things ahead."

Employee networks already existed in each of our regions when Hopson arrived and they became the platform for reducing turnover of our employees and identifying and grooming future leaders of the company. The networks were expanded into a more formalized structure that included their own budgets and regular meetings. And they became an integral part of our corporate culture—a phenomenon that I believe accounts for a good deal of our continuing success today.

Shift to Diversity

Another change we made internally was changing the name of our department from Affirmative Action to Diversity. It seemed like a small thing, but Rogercarole Rogers, Ron Brown, and I, among others, spent a great deal of time discussing the change with Hopson.

"I was never in favor, initially, of this thing called 'diversity,'" Hopson recalls today. "We needed some affirmative action to take people who had been left out and move them ahead in the company, but they finally convinced me to change the name. And when we did, people told me that it was the best thing I'd ever done. People just went along with 'affirmative action' because they had to, but they could buy into 'diversity' because that meant everybody. And I came around, too."

It was fascinating to see the process develop into a self-fulfilling prophecy as the years went by. So many of the employees who got the ball rolling made a transition that was part of the company's legacy—they became owner/operators themselves. This included early pioneers within the company like Roland Jones, Carl Osborne, Reggie Webb, and Cosmo Williams.

Meanwhile, we initially had numeric goals for our home office departments and regions—you have to go from here to there in terms of women and minority employees. But once you get sufficient numbers of people in the pipeline, the process itself takes over. Rather than pushing to get people into the system, your focus shifts to getting them ready for their next position, and the position after that. And they serve as role models for the rest of the people joining the system.

Mike Thompson clearly remembers the value of the Black Employee Network as he began his personal adjustment to working in a very large organization. "The network was key for me to be able to connect with other black professionals in McDonald's from different areas," Thompson says. "It was good because it was an uncensored way of communicating. There were goals and objectives in those networks that were designed to help employees and help the issues of diversity overall."

For Thompson, as so many others, networking combined with the training programs was a powerful combination.

Diversity in Suppliers

Early in his career with McDonald's, Thompson was one of the employees who helped bring minority suppliers into McDonald's fold—a story that starts with the NBMOA, as Lee Dunham, the first African American owner/operator in Manhattan recalls it.

Dunham—whose wife, Linda, currently serves as chair of Ronald McDonald House Charities—grew up in the mill town of Kannapolis, North Carolina. He had an entrepreneurial streak that started with a shoe-shining business when he was nine and extended to a home-remodeling business even while he served as a New York police officer. After a year-and-a-half wait for a restaurant, Dunham was asked in 1972 to introduce the first McDonald's in New York City with a franchise at 215 West 125th Street, next to the Apollo Theater in Harlem. Dunham hired former buddies from the police force as his security force to control gang activity and he was soon running the highest volume restaurant in the country and was to add seven more units to his chain.

In 1982, Dunham was approached to become the president of the NBMOA, and the first thing he did was assemble the African

American leadership and put together a 12-point agenda. "These 12 points spoke to all the things we wanted to do in the next four years," Dunham says. "And one of the most important was bringing black suppliers into the system. If it wasn't for NBMOA, McDonald's would not be where it is today because we pushed the envelop for all diversity. McDonald's right now is one of the most diverse companies in the world."

As Thompson recalls, the unique aspect of McDonald's quest for minority suppliers was that the motivation for it came from within. "This was a step that McDonald's took because it was the right thing to do and we had people with social consciences pushing the agenda," Thompson says. "Today, you see other companies making huge progress, but McDonald's was the first, and I think that McDonald's did it best."

Creating Niches

Ron Damper, a former vice president with Bankers Trust in Chicago who had resigned to start his own consulting business, became McDonald's first national minority supplier in 1984. In those early days, it was all about creating niches within McDonald's supply chain itself that newly formed companies could fill.

"McDonald's started by looking for existing minority companies, but since there were none that could supply McDonald's on the scale it needed, McDonald's took the initiative to find the right people and create something," Damper recalls. "They had several projects that did not compete against existing suppliers, and one of those was a national tea program."

So Damper partnered with the Victor Coffee Company in Boston, where over a year's time he learned the tea business, purchased spare equipment, and set up shop in a Chicago incubation center to create a McDonald's tea brand for both hot tea and iced tea. But that was just the start, as Damper recalls.

"Then I had to go out and win the business in each of the regions of McDonald's," Damper says. "It was quite a trial when you think about it, because we had to travel around the country and go in front of maybe 18 or 20 purchasing committees." Damper's colleagues in several other areas went through the same process in search of enough scale to make their business viable.

"Ultimately, it was a success for McDonald's, because in time the tea company, the sausage company, the crouton company, and others all came in succession," Damper says. "The owner/operators saw that McDonald's was serious about the fact that they would go out and find suppliers, or they would help create them if they couldn't find them. It was also important for McDonald's image in the community and significant to show that there was a commitment and that there could be successes."

Just as many McDonald's employees later become franchisees, there is also crossover into the supplier community. Thompson, for example, ultimately became president of one of the original minority supplier companies, and Bob Beavers is now a napkin supplier to McDonald's and in the process of establishing other companies as well.

Beavers can also look back to Dunham's aggressive agenda of "to do" items, which included the recommendation that McDonald's add an African American to its Board of Directors, for his appointment to McDonald's board. "It was a great opportunity and an honor and I felt like I carried the weight of a lot of folks on my shoulders," Beavers says. "If I failed, how would that look to the people who were looking to me to be successful to pave the way for them?" It turned out not to be an issue, as Beavers served 27 years on McDonald's Board before stepping down when he left the company to become a supplier.

A Fight for More Balance

The NBMOA made a concerted effort in the 1990s that further established the credibility of diversity within McDonald's, though it was a tough issue for both McDonald's and the NBMOA to resolve. Through the years, the NBMOA had grown to be a powerful network of African American owner/operators within the system and they started a movement to achieve the same representation within the system with other franchisees. What happened next illustrates the unique way McDonald's relates to its owner/operator community.

Having primarily joined the system to run restaurants in the inner city, McDonald's African American franchisees hadn't kept pace with the growth of their suburban counterparts, either in terms of numbers of restaurants owned or sales volumes. As Dunham puts it, "We stayed in those confined areas because people would say, 'there's gold in them there ghettoes, and we need some folks who can bring it out.'"

Mines saw the NBMOA begin to change as it dealt with these concerns. "The NBMOA evolved from a militant group working from the outside to one of the top franchise groups inside McDonald's," Mines says. "There's an inner and outer circle, and when you're on the outside circle, you're always outside looking in. But if you make it to the inner circle, you're always looking out, and the NBMOA has become most effective as it has moved to the inner circle."

Webb, who by this point had become an owner/operator, agrees. "The NBMOA originally had been organized like a civil rights group, and we needed to do less of that and more as a business group."

The effort to address this issue in earnest began when Fran Jones was president of the NBMOA in the late 1980s. Jones, one of 14 children raised in Baltimore, was working as an operations manager for in-flight services for United Airlines in San Francisco when she interviewed with Reggie Webb—then the regional manager in Los Angeles—about joining McDonald's as a franchisee. Her first restaurant was located in Ojai, California, a community with no African American presence at the time.

After a rocky beginning, which included death threats and special security, Jones turned that restaurant around and ultimately added three more stores to her business. And she would always be impressed by a visit she received from Dunham soon after she opened that first restaurant.

"Lee was president of the NBMOA at that time," Jones says, "I was so impressed with the mission of the network and the fact that an operator would come across the country to visit a new operator in their restaurant. Diane Peoples and I became the first two women to sit on the board of the NBMOA and some males had concerns about female leadership, so I went from the racial to the sexual tension."

As president of the NBMOA, Jones took complaints from her fellow African American operators to heart, but she knew that it would take more than anecdotal evidence to persuade the corporation to act. So she worked exhaustively to develop the facts behind the business case for more balance, and that became the starting point for negotiations with the company.

Two-Way Dialogue

"What's important to recognize is that a corporation the size of McDonald's listened, and things got done," Jones recalls. "Did we have to find the facts? Yes, we did, and I don't think it's because they didn't want to know them. When you have a corporation as large as McDonald's with such a diverse group of people each running their own separate operations, the people at the top don't always know what's going on. So it took all of us collectively, with other McDonald's people, to pull that information together."

"I'll never forget the day when I presented to Ed Rensi, the head of McDonald's USA, and he said to me, 'You're absolutely right. We will make a change.' We are embraced. We don't do this as adversaries, we do this as partners, and I don't think there's another corporation in this country that compares with us."

Hearing the facts made a strong impression on Rensi and his right-hand man, Tom Dentice. "I walked out of that room and was nearly in tears," Rensi recalls. "I told Tom that they have been our friends for 30 years and everything they said is the truth. And Tom said the problem isn't going to get solved until we tell these operators that we agree with them and they've been treated badly. So that's what we did."

Despite that initial agreement, it took a long time and many negotiations to pin down the specific program and timeline that would resolve the issue. The idea of balance meant that African American franchisees should own the same proportionate numbers of restaurants, with comparable sales volumes, as their white counterparts. The resolution finally came when Reggie Webb was chairman of the NBMOA and led a delegation of 18 of the most successful African American operators in a meeting with McDonald's top executives.

"When we went into the room to talk to McDonald's and the 19 of us showed up, McDonald's knew we were serious," Webb recalls. "The people that had the least to gain were the ones that were risking the most for the people who had the most to gain. That was a big move, both within the NBMOA for unity and as an expression of that unity to McDonald's."

"The Same Opportunity"

"We didn't want more, we just wanted the same opportunity as everybody else, and that's what the agreement at its essence defined. It took a year and a half to negotiate the agreement and then three years to bring the agreement to life," says Webb.

When the agreement was complete, some 600 additional restaurants had been sold to African American operators to bring them into a fair balance with the rest of the system. Today, the NBMOA represents some 325 owner/operator entities owning some 1,500 restaurants doing about $3.5 billion in annual sales. Collectively, our African American owner/operators, if they were considered as a separate entity, would represent one of the largest black business organizations in the country.

Larry Triplett, a restaurant owner in the San Francisco Bay Area, was the NBMOA president when the agreement was completed. As he recalls, "To McDonald's credit, they engaged in dialogue with us, and I think it helped the company because those who made the decision actually strengthened the company."

Earning Recognition

So, throughout the process of embracing diversity at McDonald's with our African America franchisees, employees, and suppliers, we benefited from the application of the three fundamental principles that are the foundation of diversity—strong management support at the top, training and education, and networking. And the last two factors reinforce each other from the individual employee standpoint, as Rogercarole Rogers points out.

"The classes give the individuals in a network the intellectual basis to understand why the network is necessary," she says. "And then the network continues to empower them to understand what they can achieve, it gives them the role models, and it gives them a voice to management, a conduit."

But there's one additional factor that can come into play after you've done all that, and that is outside recognition, which is the icing on the cake.

When Mel Hopson began training me to take over his leadership role in the department, he said one of the most important things to do was to make sure McDonald's accomplishments were known and appreciated by the outside world.

We were making good progress internally at the time, but Hopson pointed out that, when people outside of McDonald's recognized us, that meant something special because it was external validation. In other words, you could talk about how good you were all you wanted, but talk was cheap. When someone outside your organization said you were doing a good job, that really meant something because they didn't have an ulterior motive.

So that served as the basis for a lot of the work we did, and continue to do today, to build relationships with organizations outside McDonald's. It was really the same philosophy that McDonald's restaurants used to build their business in their neighborhoods—get involved with community leaders, work on common projects, and build your business as you strengthen your community.

Building Brand Value

We began to work in earnest in building our brand value and sustainable partnerships within the African American community through our participation in such national organizations as the National Urban League, the National Association for the Advancement of Colored People, the Rainbow/PUSH Coalition, and many other groups, including local community organizations.

This participation creates a two-way flow of communications that helps all of us. By being active members of these groups, we not only build personal relationships, we also provide a window into McDonald's and our commitment to diversity. Many outside people are often surprised to learn what we are like at first, but they come to see over time that we have created a sustaining, ongoing diversity ethic within the company, and they relay this information to others.

At the same time, when there might be controversy boiling up from a local source, our contacts within these organizations alert us at an early stage and help us deal with whatever the situation might be. That's an immense help to us, because we can then solve the problem before it takes on a life of its own.

These are the kinds of relationships that have to be built over time, not just when you're in a crisis. And you must have a long-term record of commitment within your own organization to justify the trust that you ask others to place in you.

The first job is always to make sure your own house is in order, and then you can be sure that whatever honors or recognition might come your way are justified. If you try to shortcut that process by seeking to gain positive recognition first, you will find out that a good reputation is short lived.

Powerful Vindication

The power of diversity and being a good citizen in the community sometimes shows itself in dramatic and unexpected ways. And the story of what happened to McDonald's during the riots in Los Angeles following the Rodney King verdict in April of 1992 is one that's hard to believe, true though it is.

Those terrible events in Los Angeles resulted in looting, arson, and vandalism that caused an estimated $2 billion in damage to local businesses in the area, 53 deaths, and more than 2,000 people injured. But, in the heart of all that destruction, the rioters spared the local McDonald's restaurants—restaurants that were owned and operated by local African American entrepreneurs and members of the community. Here's how *Time* magazine described the scene:

> When the smoke cleared after the mobs burned through South Central Los Angeles, hundreds of businesses, many of them black-owned, had been destroyed.
>
> Yet not a single McDonald's restaurant had been touched.
>
> The Los Angeles experience was vindication of enlightened social policies begun more than three decades ago.
>
> As a result, McDonald's stands out not only as one of the more socially responsible companies in America, but also as one of the nation's truly effective social engineers.

The secret to what many considered a miracle was not really a secret at all, as you've read in the preceding pages. It was the result of our commitment to diversity and being part of the fabric of the community—not just in words, but also in deeds.

Beavers was one of the first McDonald's officers on the scene to observe what happened firsthand. "We toured the area and saw the businesses that were burnt down and ripped apart and then, all of a sudden, there's a McDonald's," Beavers remembers. "McDonald's was still operating and we saw that in neighborhood after neighborhood."

The Extra Step

"It was a very clear indication that the franchisees had embraced the community and people knew who they were and what they stood for and just left them alone," Beavers recalls. "It was important to reflect the community, but those franchisees went the extra step. There were things that they did with the local churches and community organizations that let the community know they were willing to walk the walk. They didn't just talk a good game, they lived it."

As Beavers says, those McDonald's restaurants were owned by the people in the community, they hired employees from the community, earned the loyalty of customers in the community, and reached out to support the community in a number of different ways.

J.C. Gonzalez-Mendez, who today is president of our Latin America business, was an operations manager for about 100 company-owned restaurants during the riots. He concurs that being completely spared from any damage clearly demonstrates what a commitment to diversity means to the community. He says, "People believe that you do not mess around where my son works, or with what my neighbor owns, or where my wife eats. It's just a testament to what McDonald's has been able to do."

In fact, our response to the devastation itself demonstrated our concern for the community. Our local restaurants provided more than 10,000 meals to fire fighters, police officers, and the National Guard in the days following the riots. Our suppliers, whose trucks couldn't get through the riot-blocked streets, set up pick-up depots where restaurants could retrieve products to serve their customers.

One of our local operators, Harold Patrick, remembers the response when they delivered Happy Meals to a local school the following Monday. "The kids cheered when they saw the food," he said.

Fran Jones, another local operator who served breakfast to weary firemen during the ordeal, said, "Throughout the crisis, a genuine human spirit came alive. We helped each other. And we saw that our relationships in the community mean something to people."

This determination to reflect the communities we serve helps us gain the support of the people in all our communities throughout the country. It happens in less dramatic ways, but it takes place every day of the year because of our commitment to diversity.

Benchmarking

In a similar way, Beavers once told me that our work would be properly recognized when we became a benchmark company for diversity. We will know we've arrived when other companies are coming to us and asking, "How did you do it?"

And that's where we have arrived today, even though we know we still have a lot more to do ourselves.

Years ago, IBM was a benchmark company for us. Ted Childs, my good friend and now-retired counterpart at IBM, brought us in and showed us their approach. And, while some of the things they did are different from our approach, we learned many things at IBM that we applied to our work at McDonald's.

And now we're happy to serve as a benchmark for many, many companies that have come into McDonald's to study and learn from our diversity efforts. We've worked with Coca-Cola, Walgreen's, Tyson Foods, Applebee's, and many others. And I've found that you can always learn something new from others, even when they're looking to learn from your experience.

As Ron Brown says, "Somebody wants to know where I've seen this work and I send them to McDonald's. Other companies come in and they see a huge gap between what McDonald's has accomplished and where they're starting from or where they are."

Work Is Never Done

Creating a diverse workforce is a process that's never finished, and we know that we have to work at it each and every day. That's why I used Ray Kroc's quotation as the title of this book: "None of us is as good as all of us."

Our experience in embracing African Americans in our business helped us develop our overall approach to diversity, although there were some differences in the way we brought women into the organization.

Lessons Learned

Growing the diversity of our organization through the inclusion of African American leadership in our three-legged stool of owner/operators, suppliers, and employees taught us the importance of training and education.

McDonald's was a training organization from the outset, and we knew the benefits of teaching people how to run successful restaurants the McDonald's way. We knew how to train new crew members in the routines of preparing food and serving customers in our restaurants, and we knew how to train franchisees and store managers to run the business. It was this commitment to training that created the consistency of the McDonald's experience in our restaurants.

But we discovered that training in the techniques of our business was not enough to make diversity work within the organization. We needed to apply what we knew about training to broader issues, about society both outside and inside of the corporation.

While we were successful in bringing people of color into McDonald's in the early years, we were not as successful in keeping them. Prospects we brought into McDonald's did not understand what it took to succeed and be productive within a corporate culture, whether it was ours or anybody else's. And we did not understand how to manage people whose background and experience was so different from ours.

That's when we realized that we had to apply what we knew about training and education to bridge the gap of understanding. We needed to give people the tools to understand the corporate culture and operate successfully within our structure. In our case, it was the Black Career Development courses that helped our employees understand what McDonald's was all about and how to chart a successful career path within our culture. In many cases, what were perceived as "racial" barriers were actually challenges that faced all employees, regardless of color.

At the same time, we created courses on managing diversity for our existing managers to help them understand that our diversity efforts were not just about meeting numbers, but making the most of the diverse backgrounds and experiences of all the new people coming into McDonald's. As we have seen, these courses were as eye-opening for many of our existing managers as the career development courses were for our African American employees.

What does this mean for you as you look at diversity practices within your organization?

It's clear that diversity takes more than good intentions and recruitment of minorities to be successful. You have to make sure that you provide the training and education that people need so they have the tools and understanding to be successful after they've won the job. And you also need to help your existing managers understand how they need to change and adapt their practices to assure that you tap all the diverse talent that you're bringing into the organization.

Training and education provide the foundation for making diversity work for you. If you skip that vital step, you'll find out what we did in our early days—instead of opening the door to opportunity, you're only providing a revolving door for your minority employees.

5

The Women's Experience

$\mathcal{T}$op management commitment, training, and networking played an important role in the emergence of women within McDonald's, just as they did for African Americans. However, the evolution of women as a part of McDonald's diversity took a somewhat different path from the African American experience for several different reasons.

Lillian "Mickey" McMahon, the former owner of an advertising agency whose office was on the same floor as McDonald's, became the first woman to own a franchise on her own, opening a restaurant in Pontiac, Michigan in 1960. Ray Kroc came to know Mickey by walking down the hall to borrow her phone when his own office was overwhelmed by calls.

Her son, Jack McMahon, now owns four restaurants of his own in Michigan. He recalls how his mother got that first franchise:

"When my Mom asked Ray if she could become a partner with someone else in owning a restaurant, he said, 'You don't need a partner.' She didn't. And at that time there was a long waiting list to get a franchise, but when my mom's time came, Ray even picked out a location for her."

McMahon was an exception, however, because women were rarely considered franchisee material in the early days. In fact, many women were involved in the management of McDonald's restaurants with their husbands from the outset, but they weren't listed as "official" franchisees.

Another factor that distinguished women's emergence within McDonald's was the fact that there was not a compelling business reason to add them to the company's demographic approach to selling hamburgers. Unlike African Americans or Hispanics, they did not represent ethnic minorities who provided a face to

McDonald's ownership in a local community where those citizens lived and worked. This thinking gradually changed as it became clear that women—particularly mothers of young children—made so many crucial decisions about patronizing McDonald's. The company realized that making sure there was a woman's point of view represented by its owner/operators, employees, and suppliers would help its restaurants become more welcoming to female customers.

A Late Start

Finally, considering the general exclusion of women from working in McDonald's restaurants in the early years, women got a late start in finding job opportunities within the structure of restaurant operations. In a company where experience and knowledge of the unique way we managed our restaurants was essential to promotions, there were simply no women working their way through the pipeline for many years. And because women were not a strong force in the franchising community for such a long time, there was not as much pressure for change being exerted by women owner/operators as there would be down the road.

I should also note that, even though I am discussing the development of our diversity efforts for African Americans, women, Hispanics and others in separate chapters, these initiatives were all taking place at more or less the same time. Individual activities often overlapped and they all took place in an atmosphere of intensive growth in our overall business itself.

So, if it seems somewhat hectic and confusing looking back upon these events today, that's exactly how it seemed to all of us at the time.

The Pioneers

After June Martino's key role in the creation of McDonald's, Marge Cooke and Bonnie Kos became McDonald's first two female officers and they—along with Monica Boyles—played important roles in changing the environment for women within McDonald's.

Cooke grew up in a typical household in Chicago at the time— her father was an engineer and her mother was a full-time home-maker. "My father would not tolerate the idea of my mother going to work," Cooke remembers. "That was a sign of the times, I guess."

Cooke was working as a secretary for Bell and Howell when her unit was about to be eliminated, so she took a secretarial position at McDonald's working for Ray Kroc. It was here that she met her husband, John Cooke, who was an executive assistant for Kroc and later became head of Human Resources. She ultimately worked in a similar position for Fred Turner, who was ascending to the top position in the company at the time.

Kos was hired in 1970 to work on special projects, and she found herself in a rapidly expanding company that was constructing a new office building and trying to do 50 things at once. "It was shocking in a way," Kos says. "The second day I was there, they told me that there was a meeting at IBM and I should go over there and find out what word processing was and decide if we needed it. That's how we made decisions.

"The company was growing so fast and our people were totally focused on real estate and operations. They just wanted all this other stuff to happen because they didn't have time to think about how we were going to grow and where we were going to put people and how much it was going to cost."

Boyles joined the company in 1971 in the Labor Relations unit of Personnel and then worked on the restaurant business when the company finally began employing women in that area.

"There was a lot of conversation about that in the company because people were afraid that hiring women in restaurant man-agement was going to create chaos," Boyles recalls. "At that time, we were still doing things in the restaurants that required a lot of manual dexterity and heavy lifting and some people thought we just would not be capable of doing the physical work. Others were worried about what would happen if you had women and men working together in the restaurants, particularly at night."

By 1977, the company was already spilling out of its new home office at the Plaza Building in Oak Brook, Illinois and both Kos and Cooke found themselves working with Turner on plans for a new Office Campus on a 101-acre Oak Brook site the company had purchased.

In the wide-ranging discussions that went on during those meetings, Kos and Cooke would often complain that, even though the company had hired women in support jobs in Human Resources and Accounting, there were none in Operations, where the big decisions were made, according to Kos.

Women in the Pipeline?

"Fred kept saying, 'No, there are women in the pipeline,' and Marge and I would say that they weren't there, they kept getting sabotaged," Kos says. "So Fred told us, and this was really incredible in his insight, he told us to gather all the operations women that we knew and bring them in for a day so they could tell him what their problems were."

Cooke and Kos filled a conference room, and Boyles was there as one of just eight woman restaurant managers at the time. As the women began to talk, they told some terrible horror stories about the way they were being treated. And Turner, who has three daughters, was "beside himself" as Kos remembers it, so he told Cooke and Kos that he wanted the problem fixed.

"When Fred started this process, Bonnie and I didn't get along very well; we tended to go our own separate ways," Cooke recalls. "But he put the two of us together to work on the project and I always felt he did it because Bonnie was the mouthy one and I tended to be quieter."

Together, they brought in Boyles to head a department called "Managing the Changing Workforce" and decided that this was a situation in which the company needed to look outside for help, so they turned to a niche consulting firm that was part of Boyle Kirkman, based in New York. The consultants were already doing this kind of affirmative action training, according to Malou Roth, who ultimately came in to do training sessions for McDonald's. The fact that an outside firm was invited to work with McDonald's people was very unusual at that time.

"Against Consultants"

"We almost fell on the floor when we got the okay, because Fred Turner was against using any consultants at McDonald's," Kos says. "He always said you have to force yourself to run your own company and not rely on consultants, and he was real smart about that. But he was very impressed with them and their plan, even when they said that he had to be in charge, not Human Resources, not another woman."

So Turner became the head of what he called the "Women's Lib Committee" and took on the challenge. Years later he would say, "When I went home and told my daughters I was the chairman of the Lib Committee, they started laughing, and they haven't stopped yet. I was kind of ticked off—I was proud of it and I didn't understand why they thought it was so funny."

The program started with a presentation at a national conference in 1979 called Operations Homecoming, which introduced the idea of better utilizing women and minorities in the company. "People were enamored by the questions she [Barbara Boyle] asked," Boyles says. "She made them think without making them feel stupid, but she called out the need for more knowledge and created a call from the system for more information."

But the presentation was just the start of the process. The heart of the proposal was a two-pronged training program—one for all managers in the company and then one for training the women employees.

"The manager's program was really the big one because we were talking about every single manager in the company," Roth says. "It worked well because Fred Turner was active and involved, and Marge Cooke was in charge as our 'go-to' person. It's a good example of how an executive can sponsor something and it doesn't take a lot of his time—he or she just has to be hovering around and others have to know he or she is in the background."

Kos remembers that Turner would respond to regional managers who would say their people didn't have time for classes and wouldn't participate by calling them up personally. "Fred would say, 'why don't you want to come to my class?' " Kos says. "That's how he put it—why don't you want to come to *my* class?"

And the fact that Cooke, who had worked so closely with Turner in the past, was in charge made a big difference, too, according to Roth. "These were general managers who weren't scared of anything," Roth says. "But they were scared of Fred and scared of getting turned in. And the theory Fred had was that you can believe what you want but we're going to operate differently now. They were going to have to set aside some of their beliefs because it's very hard to have one set of beliefs, yet act differently. So we were forcing people into a new paradigm by making them take a look at what they were doing."

Kos agrees that there was no wavering in Turner's position. "Fred led the charge the whole way," she says. "He never once backed off. He never once said that we're not going to do this. He's a fair person and he believes in diversity, so he would have done it whether he had three daughters or not."

Cooke purposely picked the five toughest regions in the country—those who had a reputation for being bastions of male chauvinism—for the first five training classes. "This was the beauty of Marge and Fred and this is why the program worked," Roth says. "Had she picked regular regions with regular people in them, we wouldn't have had the credibility. But, because we did well in those five tough regions, we got a notch in our belt and we were okay for the other places."

Train the Trainer

Turner wanted to extend the training all the way to the restaurant level, so the consultants worked with Boyles to write a "train the trainer" class and involved a cadre of McDonald's people who would carry on the program. "We came to realize fairly soon that we could do this training ourselves," Boyles recalls. "Developing this class enabled us to be self-sufficient."

Within McDonald's, the trainers came from all categories—they didn't have to be women or minorities. And, as the courses got underway in earnest, it soon became apparent that their value could extend beyond just women in the workforce, according to Boyles.

"We came to realize this was not just a gender issue," she says. "It was broader. So we connected with outside people and developed career development programs for African American and Hispanic employees, and, ultimately, we trained our own people to conduct those classes as well."

The program to train women specifically began in 1980 with week-long classes that ran through 1986. Here, also, the consultants trained additional trainers within the company, and McDonald's continued the classes after that with our own people.

Roth noticed an interesting psychological phenomenon as she conducted the training classes throughout the country. "People just assumed that their regions were the ones that were lacking, but that the other ones must have had women and blacks," she says. "The main thing we were trying to do with the classes was get people to understand how important this was to the company, that this wasn't going away, and that their internal workforce had to mirror their outside customers, which was a concept that they had never thought about before. We saw changes. McDonald's had some goals, and they had to start hiring and promoting women and minorities. They walked out of these classes realizing that life as they knew it was over, and it was."

Pipeline Swells

As the barriers to women working in McDonald's restaurant operations began to tumble, the pipeline of qualified women in the workforce began to swell—not only opening the doors to higher-ranking jobs within the company, but also creating a cadre of women who would be ready to become franchisees in their own right.

"Fred Turner and Mike Quinlan insisted that field officers and Oak Brook officers have a short list of women and African Americans at all times," Boyles remembers. "They'd walk up to them and say, 'How is so-and-so doing?,' and at every quarterly officer meeting, everybody had to come with their list of names. And Fred kept his own list, so he knew if you took somebody off or changed it . . . he knew and he would ask you about it. People were accountable and they knew it."

Chris Beck-McKay was one of those early pioneers, having taken a job with McDonald's in 1976 after graduating from Pacific Lutheran University in Tacoma, Washington with a degree in economics and business administration. She actually met her husband-to-be, Mark McKay, at her first management training course, and she ultimately became the president of the Women Operators Network (WON) in 2006.

"When I first started, I think the people I worked with thought that women were capable of doing the job, but they just weren't sure that women should be there—they were uncomfortable with the whole thing," Beck-McKay recalls. "I was the second female store manager for McOpCo [the McDonald's company-owned restaurants] in the Seattle Region, and they would have their store manager meetings at a strip club called 'My Place.' Needless to say, they went without me. It was a mindset that you're not really one of the guys."

After they were married, the McKays worked their way through the staff jobs for the company, and when they expressed an interest in becoming owner/operators, they were offered a chance to buy into a partnership in five restaurants in Salt Lake City in 1988, ultimately buying out the company's half in 1991. Today, they own and operate seven restaurants.

"The Women Operators Network started in 1988, and I went to a couple of meetings, but I'd be lying if I didn't tell you that our entire focus was on our restaurants," she says. "We worked six full days every week and didn't take vacations. There's a spotlight on you as a woman, and you want to make sure your restaurants are operating at an excellent level before you do anything else."

Establishing a Network

This feeling by women that they had to prove themselves as competent operators first and foremost actually led to a slow start in the initial formation of the WON. At Turner's urging, Boyles and Cooke identified women operators from around the country who were strong and well-regarded and brought them to Chicago for a meeting.

"The whole idea was to get them to form a group and we would pay for it if they would do it," Boyles recalls. "There was a lot of energy and excitement, but then they all went home and nothing happened. We'd call another meeting and they'd come, but in between meetings nothing would happen. That went on for several years."

Marilyn Wright, a native of Croatia, was one of the founders of the WON. She had immigrated to the United States at the age of 17, learned English, and was married to Ralph Wright, who owned a large mechanical contracting company in the Chicago area. The Wrights were initially interested in McDonald's because customers paid for their food upfront.

"We had 80 people working for us and 33 trucks on the road as contractors," Wright recalls with a laugh. "But we had a million dollars in inventory and a million dollars walking the streets in receivables, and my husband said he was tired of people not paying their bills."

After qualifying with McDonald's, they found a walk-up restaurant in Chicago for sale, made an offer, and took over the restaurant in 1976. As was the practice at the time, Ralph Wright was the approved franchisee and Marilyn was the working partner—"a ribbon on Ralph's package," as she describes it.

A decade later, the company called Wright and a few other women operators together for yet another lunch meeting to discuss an organization that could help other women acting as franchisees throughout the system. This time the idea clicked, and Darlene McKeller, an owner/operator in Arizona, became the first president of the WON.

"There were 11 of us at that meeting," Wright recalls. "I remember that because we each pitched in a hundred dollars apiece to open a bank account and we started with eleven hundred dollars. The company offered to sponsor the group but we said that we didn't need their money; we'd do it ourselves. I didn't see any need for it myself, but, as we sat down and talked to other women and started looking at the facts a little deeper, the need became more obvious."

The first challenge the fledgling WON organization tackled was the need for two documents to cover the franchise agreement— so that women who were 50-50 partners in the business could also be recognized as approved operators. In some cases, wives were running the entire restaurant organization by themselves, yet their husbands were still designated as the sole approved operator. They took on this issue with the company's franchising directors, including Burt Cohen, John Kujawa, and Gene Stachowiak, and sorted out the logistics on a case-by-case basis.

Self-Help Goal

A larger goal was to support the women operators throughout the system and show them the way to success. "We encountered a beautiful group of people in every part of the country," Wright says. "They loved working together, they loved the opportunity to advance and succeed, and they found out it's a great support group they can lean on if they have any questions or difficulties or issues."

In the process, Wright has demonstrated the power of diversity in her own operation, which has grown to 650 employees working in 15 restaurants in the Chicago area, including the flagship "Rock and Roll McDonald's" in the heart of Chicago that was rebuilt to celebrate the company's 50th anniversary in 2005.

"Mel Hopson would call me the United Nations," Wright says. "I have managers and crew from Korea, Syria, the Middle East, Mexico, Ecuador, Cuba, and Nicaragua. We came here the same way—we were foreigners, not a word of English, so you have to learn new customs, new culture, a new life, all of that. It's hard and you do need people and you do need support. You need somebody who's a role model to show you the way.

"I think the company has a huge opportunity with diversity that it needs to stay close with and put its weight and leverage behind, because that makes sure that we are reflecting our customer base out there."

Looking back, Cooke sees the WON as a catalyst for a great deal of the system's progress in including women. "The WON helped change a lot," Cooke says. "The women operators who started it were strong women and very good operators. Most of them started in the business with their husbands, but then a lot of them got stores by reason of separation or divorce and others just got good at running it and took it over.

"These were very strong women and they were good in organizing themselves into both a social and a business relationship."

Sticky Floors

Wright remembers that many people within McDonald's didn't believe that there was a glass ceiling restricting how high women could rise in the organization. "I used to say that there might not be any glass ceilings, but there were some very sticky floors in parts of the company," Wright says.

And the women operators were also able to add value to the business by providing a different perspective on our markets and customers. "We all see things so differently," says Chris Beck-McKay. "The goal can be the same, but the vision you have to get there can be so different, and that's a huge strength for McDonald's. In companies where you see only men, they may be brilliant tacticians or brilliant at making money, but they might not have the heart or compassion or passion that women can bring to the business."

Susan Chrisman, who served as the WON president from 2004 to 2005, recalls how she was allowed to fill out the application and go through the McDonald's franchisee training program in Del Rio, Texas in the late-1980s because she would be the person running the business.

"My husband, Larry, was a banker in Del Rio and I had been very active in community organizations," Chrisman says. "So when I was training by working the drive-thru window all day, everybody in town who saw me there thought Larry had lost his money in banking, which was going through a tough period at the time."

Employee Networking

Once the WON began to show the benefits of networking, the same idea took hold with our employees as well, thanks again to Cooke,

Kos, Boyles, and Vivian Ross, who had joined McDonald's as a labor relations attorney in 1978.

"I held the first meeting of our women's group in my condominium in Chicago," Ross recalls. "We sat around and talked about what we could do to help other women, and there was a consensus within this small group that women could often be each others' worst enemies. Some successful women felt they were struggling so hard they couldn't help anybody else, and others were undermining their colleagues so they could be the 'queen bee.'

"But we said that we were confident enough in ourselves and in our jobs, and we were close enough to the field and the home office, that maybe we could help, even if it was just to talk to other women who were similarly situated."

That small beginning ultimately served as a catalyst for a self-help network that women within the company could turn to for advice and mentoring.

"The company women were watching what was going on with the Women Operators Network," Boyles recalls. "It was getting a lot of energy and excitement, and the women operators were benefiting and the company was benefiting. The women employees were interested, so Marge and Bonnie and I put together an effort to help the women in the company to get together as well."

Thus, the Women's Leadership Network was born and gradually evolved into a powerful networking system, although it took a while to find itself. Johanne Luth was one of our early women employees in the field, having worked on a restaurant crew in 1972, and coming into the company in a manager trainee position in 1977.

"My first involvement with the Women's Leadership Network came when I was working as a field consultant," Luth recalls. "At the time, we just got together and socialized. I pushed hard for us to do something, but it was hard to sell change back then."

Luth later became an operator herself with four restaurants in the Bay City, Michigan area, served as the first chairwoman of the Central Division Leadership Council, and then moved to the

National Leadership Council executive team, being elected as secretary/treasurer of the owner/operator's national organization.

"At the time, I was amazed that the good-old-boy network would let two women into the leadership of the NLC, but now there are eight women involved," she says. "I feel we can accomplish anything now. Back when I started in 1977, my operations manager thought I'd be barefoot and pregnant before long."

Starts in the Regions

The value of networking comes alive more vividly in the regions and divisions, according to Maura Havenga, who started as a crew member in one of our restaurants in the 1970s and has since risen to become one of the highest ranking women executives in the company as senior vice president of Worldwide Operations & Systems in our Restaurant Solutions Group.

"Growing up in a region, you really do learn and understand the importance of networks and communication and connection and leveraging others to help you really understand the business," Havenga says. "You have fewer resources in a region or a division, so you depend more on each other and grow those relationships and networks.

"When I went to work in the home office, I found it to be very siloed, with less crossover and networking. It's been fun for me to help people get outside the box and really challenge their thinking. My vision is that networks are about self help, empowerment, and growing the business, and if you use those screens, we've only just begun to unleash the potential of the networks within the system today."

Ross says that today the women's networks have been an "amazing contribution" to the system. "One of our greatest achievements is the development of the pipeline and heightening the awareness of people to the pipeline," Ross says. "The issue of women has been taken to a whole new level."

The WLN also found a natural ally in the WON.

"The WON feels like they are responsible for always putting women in the organization in the path of getting attention and promotion," says Susan Chrisman. "A WLN member once said to me, 'What you need to do for me is to keep me in the light. Keep me in the forefront.' Because of the number of women in the company, we have to realize that, if you're going to be able to talk to women customers, you better have women riding that train."

Women in the Supply Chain

McDonald's also extends its diversity efforts to women suppliers. One of the first is Paula Marshall, a third-generation owner of Bama Pies.

The company started in the kitchen of Marshall's grandmother, Alabama Marshall, who cooked pies that were delivered to customers throughout Dallas by her seven children. Eventually, the siblings each opened a Bama Pie operation in different cities throughout the Southwest, including Houston, Waco, Shreveport, Little Rock, Tulsa, and Oklahoma City, as well as their original home base in Dallas.

"That was my grandfather's way of getting national distribution, but he just ran out of kids," Marshall says today.

Marshall's father Paul developed a fried pie that could be held in your hand and eaten, and he, having heard about Ray Kroc's success, drove to the original restaurant in Des Plaines, Illinois with samples packed in dry ice in his trunk. Kroc was interested in just such a product and told Marshall that he would put them in his restaurants all over the world, even though in 1963 Kroc had just over 500 restaurants.

"When you think back, it gives you goose bumps," Paula Marshall says today. "Two crazy guys sitting in the back of a McDonald's restaurant in 1963 having this dream, actually two dreams at once."

Bama Pies got the business, and set up production plants around the world as McDonald's was extending its international reach, until, finally, Paul Marshall decided to retire in 1984. His oldest son, who had been helping run the business, was suffering from heart problems. So he asked his daughter, Paula, if she would take over.

There was some initial reluctance from McDonald's until former McDonald's president Mike Roberts, who at that time was in charge of finding minority suppliers as part of McDonald's affirmative action program, stepped in.

"My dad didn't bat an eye," Marshall recalls. "He and my mom worked with their attorney, made all the legal changes we needed, and we became certified in 1989 as a woman-owned business enterprise.

"Along with that, McDonald's provided training for us to get better—you have to be the best you can be no matter what color or gender you are. We won the Malcolm Baldridge Quality Award because of McDonald's."

Bonnie Kos also made it a priority to use minority-owned vendors in the construction projects she oversaw through the years. "We did millions and millions of dollars worth of construction, so we put a woman-owned company in place in those areas whenever we could," Kos says. "We had more minority people than any department in the company, and more minority-owned suppliers."

Women's Foodservice Forum

McDonald's also became very involved in outside organizations supporting women, including helping to form the Women's Food-service Forum, which began with Monica Boyles's involvement in 1988. It started with a couple of informal meetings with a representative from the *Restaurant Business* magazine, according to Boyles.

"We got to know each other and decided we should get together more formally as industry professionals to share information—not company secrets, but information that would enable women to be successful in this industry," Boyles says.

"There were about 10 or 12 of us who first got together at a hotel in downtown Chicago and just talked about what was possible. We decided that we had enough to offer each other to make this a business imperative and it was something that people would pay money to belong to, because it would be the kind of information that would enable their companies to be more successful."

Boyles asked me to get involved with the group, and I was privileged to be among the founding members when the organization officially began in 1989. The Women's Foodservice Forum (WFF) today has more than 2,200 members, we attract more than 3,000 women who attend our annual conference, and the WFF is a driving force for the advancement of women in the industry.

One of the highlights of my involvement with the WFF came in 1997 when we asked Ed Rensi, then-president of McDonald's USA, to deliver the keynote speech at our annual conference. Part of the pride I felt was the many, many women Ed singled out from within McDonald's—women employees, women franchisees, and women suppliers. But the real source of inspiration to me was the message he delivered to all the women in the audience.

Message to Women

"It's important to understand the nature of our journey and the progress we've made," Rensi said. "Committing to the continued development and advancement of women in the industry is a path we must walk every day. It's not a destination we reach.

"Diversity means opportunity, and when opportunity knocks, someone has to answer. That's where the Women's Foodservice Forum can help you. The Forum delivers the educational experience that strengthens your leadership talent and your practical skills. This gets you ready to answer opportunity's knock.

"This isn't about the individual reaching the top of their organization; it's about reaching your potential, having the opportunity to achieve your individual goals, and being able to make the individual choice to aspire to the very top positions."

Many members of McDonald's have served in leadership positions with the WFF, including Sue Warzecka, former senior vice president for McDonald's USA; my former colleague, Chere Nabor, who was senior director of diversity for many years; Paula Marshall, president of Bama Foods; and our current board representative, Vivian Ross, vice president of labor relations; among many others through the years.

Catalyst for Women

Boyles and Cooke also developed a relationship with the Catalyst organization and its founder, Felice Schwartz. Our CEO at the time, Mike Quinlan, joined the Catalyst board as a demonstration of our support.

"Catalyst was very small then, but Felice thought that women were being underutilized in business and she wanted companies that were working hard at this to work with her to either prove out what she thought or not," Boyles says. "So McDonald's, General Electric, and a number of other major companies worked with her and clearly were able to prove what she initially thought was true."

Catalyst began honoring innovative approaches with proven results by organizations addressing women's issues in business, and we were very proud when the McDonald's Women Operators Network won the Catalyst Award in 1994. Once again, as Mel Hopson always told me, you really arrive when others recognize your progress.

Around the World

So, despite a late start, women have made tremendous progress in bringing their diversity, including their unique points of view, to the forefront at McDonald's. Again, the formula for success has been the constant commitment to leadership support, training and education, and networking.

And, as I'll discuss in my final chapter, we are taking the advancement of women within McDonald's to a global level as our next challenge in the continuing evolution of diversity.

Lessons Learned

Networks are a natural outgrowth of training and education—a way to extend the individual's learning progress at the same time that they can draw on the support and encouragement of their peers.

Some networks seem to appear spontaneously and grow organically. In McDonald's case, our African American owner/operators and our women employees formed informal self-support groups early on, leading the way to more formal organizations as their numbers grew.

In other cases, networks need to be nurtured and encouraged. As we saw in this chapter, the corporation tried to spur interest in a network of women franchisees several times before the idea finally caught on. Ironically, the Women Operators Network has not only evolved to become one of our largest and most active franchisee networks, but it is the only one that has chosen to financially support itself solely with its own member dues.

However networks arise, our experience at McDonald's tells us that networks are an essential tool in fostering diversity and helping employees become successful. They are not for every employee, so participation should be voluntary. But there is nothing more valuable to people facing challenges or barriers in the workplace than turning to colleagues with similar experiences for advice and counsel. A network provides a forum for finding solutions when you don't know where to turn within your own department or business unit.

At McDonald's, we help our networks function both financially and with organizational resources because we think our visible support sends a message to employees that we support the concept of networks. We believe that if a network helps create better, more satisfied employees, then it is ultimately good for us.

If you support strong networks to support the diversity of people within your organization, you will also find another benefit over time—you will become a better, stronger organization. Our networks at McDonald's provide a two-way line of communication between senior management and individuals within our diversity groups that has become a powerful way to assure the alignment of our efforts.

It is obviously a great benefit to employees—and in our case, franchisees—to be able to have direct access to what management is thinking about our strategies and tactics. That helps everyone know what they should do to succeed and help the company succeed.

But it is just as powerful for our network members to be able to express their thoughts and ideas about what is happening in our business to senior management. Many times, issues are brought to the surface at an early stage when they can be resolved before they simmer over into problems. Often, our networks identify opportunities for our business to grow that might otherwise have gone unnoticed.

So my advice is to support the networks you have in place and make sure they provide value to their individual members. And if you don't have any networks today, then seek out potential leaders within your own ranks and help create them.

6

Hispanic Americans . . . and More

*H*aving established a positive pattern that worked, McDonald's was able to use that same playbook as it opened its doors to Hispanic Americans and other minorities, including people with disabilities, Asian Americans, and the gay and lesbian community.

There were a few Hispanic employees even back in the early days of McDonald's. In fact, when I joined the company's Legal department in my first secretarial position, one of the attorneys I worked with was Santiago Rios, our first Hispanic officer.

The first Hispanic to become an owner/operator of one of our restaurants was Henry Garcia, a former U.S. Army Ranger who subsequently owned his own gas station and then worked for the Los Angeles County Flood Control District. He bought his first restaurant in 1971. Garcia had read an article in the *Wall Street Journal* about how McDonald's and other companies were looking to bring minorities into their operations and sent a letter to Oak Brook expressing his interest.

It took Garcia more than two years to save his money and complete his training. Then, McDonald's called and asked if he would take a restaurant in the Echo Park area of Los Angeles. He immediately agreed, and when he got off the phone, he asked his wife, Rosemary, "Where's Echo Park?"

The neighborhood turned out to be a high crime area with a lot of gang activities and many boarded-up buildings. The restaurant itself only had sales of $480,000 in its most recent year of operation.

"Getting involved in the community built up our sales more than anything else," Garcia recalls. "I customized my service to our Hispanic customers, including the introduction of McDonald's first bilingual menu and bottles of hot sauce on every table. We turned that operation around and were able to purchase our second store in 1974."

Leveraging Diversity

McDonald's had learned from its African American experience that the best way to serve customers in a primarily minority area was to leverage the cultural knowledge and community ties of franchisees who mirrored the neighborhoods they served. So the company began to seek out Hispanic owner/operators to serve the rapidly growing Hispanic American markets around the country.

In 1977, Rios called Garcia on the phone to suggest forming a network of Hispanic operators similar to the National Black McDonald's Operators Association. Jose Canchola and Paul Gutierrez joined Garcia in putting the groups together.

"There were 13 Hispanic operators around the country at that time, and we reached out to all of them to describe what our purpose would be," Garcia recalls. "Our idea was to be an organization that would help each other be successful in running our restaurants and our businesses."

The first official meeting of the McDonald's Hispanic Operators Association (MHOA) was held in Albuquerque, New Mexico in 1978 and featured a keynote address by Jerry Apodaca, then-Governor of New Mexico. Like the NBMOA, the MHOA's early activities focused on helping new Hispanic operators understand how to be successful in the McDonald's system, and just last year the organization celebrated its 30th anniversary.

Hispanics on Wall Street

The first Hispanic operator to open a restaurant outside of a minority neighborhood was Roberto Madan, who had immigrated to the United States as a Cuban refugee in 1960. When he first arrived in America, a friend of his took him to a "typical American restaurant"—McDonald's—to celebrate.

"When I walked into that McDonald's, I remember watching the manager sporting a crew cut and a wearing a short-sleeved shirt and everything in the restaurant was so clean," Madan recalls. "I don't know why, but I turned to my wife and I said, 'It would be nice to own one of these.'"

Madan moved to Philadelphia and worked in a factory, then became a teacher, but he always set something aside from his earnings to fulfill his dream of buying a McDonald's. Finally, when affirmative action started in the 1970s, Madan had enough money to become a silent investor with another owner/operator and he began working as a restaurant manager even as he continued teaching school.

When African American and Hispanic operators began pushing to open stores in nonminority areas, Madan was chosen to be the pioneer for the Hispanic operators, based on his experience in the restaurants. His first restaurant opened in 1979 at the corner of Fulton and Pearl Street in New York's Wall Street area. The store was only doing $800,000 in annual sales and, while Madan held onto his teaching job, he learned a valuable lesson.

"Although my first experience was not very good, McDonald's gave me that opportunity because I was Hispanic, and I saw that the opportunity was great," Madan says. "To me, affirmative action wasn't about forcing employers to meet a set of numbers; it was all about opportunity—give an Hispanic the opportunity and you will see the results."

By the early 1980s, many members of the MHOA were discouraged that not enough progress was being made and were considering dismantling their owner/operator network. Garcia asked them to suspend deliberations and took Madan outside the meeting room to ask him if he would consider being president of the organization.

"I didn't feel I could be president because a majority of the members were Mexican, but Henry Garcia said he would guarantee the support of the Mexican operators," Madan recalls. "That's how I became president, and since then we have been working together, but I did change the approach of the group."

Looking for Opportunity

"They had been pushing for numbers—more Hispanics here, more Hispanics there—and I changed that totally," Madan continues. "I just wanted an opportunity for one . . . put one Hispanic in any position and you will see the results. Then you can decide how many more you need. You put the right amount of people in and you're both going to benefit—McDonald's and Hispanics."

Isabelle Villasenor is another pioneer as an owner/operator, having wound up with a restaurant that her ex-husband's parents had owned after a divorce in 1981. "It was a bit of a burden at the time because I had more hurdles to cross being a woman, a divorcee, and a Latina," Villasenor recalls. "I needed to prove who I was if I wanted to be an operator and support my two daughters.

"As soon as I was made aware of MHOA, I got involved to the point where I became vice president of the national organization, and I found that, while I was creating that credibility for myself as a woman and a Latina, I was being approached more by others and I was realizing the importance of diversity."

Villasenor went on to become an active member of the Women Operators Network as well, ultimately rising to be president of that national organization. "We created the process as we went along and learned what mistakes were being made and how to correct them. It just took time to appreciate the value of diversity and what it meant within the system."

And, by the way, Isabelle's two daughters—Jenny and Lisa—have graduated from college and are each McDonald's owner/operators themselves today.

Into the Employee Pipeline

Meanwhile, Hispanic employees, like women and African Americans, began to enter into the McDonald's pipeline at the restaurant level, which is the foundation of the system.

Ed Sanchez, another Cuban-born immigrant whose family escaped to the United States in 1966 when he was eight years old, grew up in Miami and started working for McDonald's as a part-time crew member while he was in high school. He became a store manager at the age of 18 and by 1982 he was an Area Supervisor. And his career began to blossom with the help of the company's diversity training.

"Rudy Mendez, who was working in the Diversity department at the time, and Mel Hopson came from the home office to talk about diversity," Sanchez recalls. "They taught us how to stand out, how to have sensitivity for other people, and how to appreciate the historical aspects of the people in the Caribbean. Planting these seeds early on had a big influence on the company. Mendez and Hopson taught me that I was different—we were all different—but there was no one correct way, just different ways. That creates a strength; you're stronger as a team than as an individual."

Sanchez' career is a case study in opportunity. He went to Puerto Rico for a year, became Managing Director in Spain, and then opened up our Portugal market before returning to the United States in 1992 and becoming Regional Manager of the then-South Florida region. Ultimately, Sanchez served as President of Latin America before becoming the president of one of McDonald's major Hispanic suppliers, Lopez Foods, based in Oklahoma City.

"It's been a history of blood, sweat, and tears," Sanchez says now in looking back on the progress of diversity within McDonald's. "We started the Hispanic Leadership Network and evolved the other employee networks. McDonald's has a clear advantage in the marketplace because of its diversity commitment—we identify with our current customers.

"In my opinion, the answer was our willingness to take risks. When you stop to think about it, each McDonald's restaurant site represents a risk that somebody took."

————————

Hispanic Training

Another early Hispanic corporate employee was Rita Alborez-Pozniak, who joined the company's relocation office in 1976 and then moved into National Contributions, which led to a staff job with the just-formed Ronald McDonald Children's Charities, known today as Ronald McDonald House Charities. Alborez-Pozniak played a key role in arranging the first career development classes for Hispanics in 1979.

"The first thing I did was try to find out where we had Hispanics, so I went all around the country and I wound up with about 26 names, which said a lot," Alborez-Pozniak recalls. "The people in the first classes couldn't get over how few of them there were, and I told them that this is what these classes are all about, that if we are going to create a climate of success for the Hispanics we have, then we have to bring in a lot more and all of you are going to help us do that."

For Catherine Sanchez, the first Hispanic employee in the Phoenix Region, those classes were eye-opening. She had started with McDonald's as a manager trainee in 1980 and became a store manager in 1983. "When I first came in, I was the only Hispanic, and it was a very tough environment," she says. "Other managers had a real hard time accepting who I was."

She was promoted to area supervisor and then to regional training manager, where she had the opportunity to bring other minorities into McDonald's. "Those Hispanic Career Development classes were some of the best things that ever happened in my life," she says now. "They helped me to analyze and see where we were. A lot of Latinos still think that, if we are doing good things, somebody will notice; we don't understand that we need to market what we're doing. HCD really brought that out."

After several tours of duty in various regions and the home office, Sanchez returned to Phoenix to become an owner/operator and now serves as the regional representative for the MHOA.

Employee Networks

Alborez-Pozniak was also in on the creation of the Hispanic Employee Network, which began as a national organization because there were not really enough Hispanics in any one region to sustain a group.

"One smart thing I did was decide there would be no president or chairman; there would be a steering committee," Alborez-Pozniak says. "My gut just told me that it could be really heady to have one person out there."

They began their activities by creating Cultural Days featuring Hispanic arts and music in the company's home office. They also organized kids' days at McDonald's for Hispanic children in foster homes in the Chicago area. Ultimately, the national network organization expanded into regions as the numbers of Hispanic employees increased dramatically.

"Networks don't just happen, especially for minorities," Alborez-Pozniak says. "People may have their buddies and interface with them when they have a problem, but they're certainly not going to spend time trying to expand or polish a network group unless somebody makes it okay. And that's what McDonald's did—they made it okay."

Dr. Ron Brown, who had done so much in establishing the Black Career Development course, brought in Hispanics from his own consulting group to help develop the Hispanic Career Development (HCD) training.

Valuing Cultural Differences

In another very significant development, now that there were several minority groups competing for McDonald's attention and corporate resources, Brown sat down with Monica Boyles to develop a training course for senior managers.

"The company kind of went by the group at first," Brown says. "The officers would say things like, 'We're working on women now, and we'll get to the blacks next.' That began to create some competitive energy because Hispanics were thinking, 'Why not now for us?'"

Brown also noticed how Ed Rensi would walk into a room of black managers for a fireside chat and the discussions would be highly spirited, with the hard questions asked and answered. But when Rensi would hold a similar session with Hispanic managers and ask for questions or issues on their mind, he was met by silence. And seeing these kinds of differences led Brown and Boyles to collaborate on creating the class that we called "Managing the Changing Workforce."

"We traveled all over the system for about two years and began to talk about cultural differences and values in a course for managers, department heads, and regional managers," Brown says. "This was leading edge, it was really bleeding edge, to begin to talk about the different expressions that come out of different cultures.

"That was a big turning point in the company. People began to understand that there's white male culture, there's Hispanic culture, there's African American culture. It isn't just that people are black or brown; they have a culture behind them. That was a major turning point into understanding people's different cultures."

The Meaning of Opportunity

By the time J.C. Gonzalez-Mendez joined McDonald's in 1984, the groundwork had been well laid for those who wished to take advantage of the opportunities. A native of Mexico, he parlayed his education as a biochemical engineer and food technologist to be our first company employee in Mexico—a purchasing manager charged to develop the supply chain for our first restaurant in the country, scheduled to open the following year.

"I was lucky, and I believe luck is when opportunity and hunger meet," says Gonzalez-Mendez. "My wife was a third-generation American born in Mexico, and we were anxious to leave the country because inflation was rampant and it was very difficult to own your own house. McDonald's provided the opportunities, and we just had to take the plunge and jump in."

After two years in Mexico, Gonzalez-Mendez came to the United States to oversee quality assurance for all of Latin America, eventually including Europe and Southeast Asia in his responsibilities. He then went to Los Angeles as a purchasing agent, where he earned his MBA and also got into the operations side of the business, rolling up his sleeves and working in the restaurants. After rising to director of operations for the Los Angeles region, he returned to Mexico as the country's first native-born president of operations.

After a stint as international relationship partner for eight Latin American countries, he returned to Chicago, where he was put in charge of supply chain for the United States and Canada until his 2008 appointment as president of the Latin America business.

A Diverse Department

He is proud that U.S. Supply Chain is one of the most diverse departments in the company, with 70 percent of his former team being female and minorities. He also is quick to point out that nearly 60 percent of the $10.4 billion that McDonald's spends every year on purchases of food and supplies goes through the hands of minority-owned businesses.

"I don't think there's another company that has embraced diversity as well as McDonald's," he says. "Early on, we realized that it was not about black or brown or white; it was about green. That's why McDonald's has been so successful. We truly understand the differences and we value them, respect them, and celebrate them. It's not only staff; it also goes with franchisees and suppliers. We don't talk about it as much as we should, but that's because we don't think talking is that important—what's important is doing."

And Gonzalez-Mendez also demonstrates the company's commitment to give back to the communities we serve by serving as board member of such organizations as the National Council of La Raza, the Mexican American Opportunity Foundation, and People with Disabilities in Chicago. "We have to put the McDonald's face out into the community so people understand diversity is on the menu at McDonald's," he says.

Active in the Community

Hispanic owner/operators are also extremely active within their own communities, though few have had as lasting an impact as Richard Castro, a franchisee with more than 20 restaurants and 1,000 employees in El Paso, Texas. A school teacher before he became a McDonald's franchisee, Castro was alarmed by the high number of Hispanic students who were dropping out of high school in his hometown and across the country. So he set out to do something about it.

Castro started a scholarship fund called Hispanic American Commitment to Education Resources, popularly known as HACER. He brought together other entities to leverage his efforts, including Ronald McDonald House Charities, the National Hispanic Scholarship Fund, McDonald's Corporation, and Hispanic owner/operators from across the country. An initial collection of donations totaling $97,000 launched the fund in 1985, providing $1,000 scholarships to high school seniors in various communities.

Today, HACER has grown to become the largest scholarship fund dedicated to Hispanic students in the entire country, it has distributed more than $12 million in scholarships to more than 14,000 Hispanic students, and it continues to grow every year.

Luis Hernandez, the most recent president of the McDonald's Hispanic Operators Association, says it's important to form alliances with outside organizations. "We have the National Council of La Raza, we have MALDEF, and they all have come to us," Hernandez says. "We have a very good and healthy relationship with them— they respect McDonald's and they like McDonald's. You've got to do things for people who can't do it for themselves, and that's what these organizations do."

———————

From UPS to McDonald's

Hernandez, a native of Puerto Rico, came to McDonald's after working for 25 years with United Parcel Service, where he became their first Hispanic vice president. But he had always harbored the desire to own a McDonald's since he first visited a restaurant in 1968, so he finally took the plunge in 1996 by buying a McDonald's in a Wal-Mart in Waxahachie, Texas.

"Everybody laughed at me because I didn't have a 'real' restaurant, but there was an offer of a free-standing restaurant six months later and I wanted to be an owner," Hernandez says. "Today, I have nine restaurants."

Hernandez focused on his restaurants in his early years with the system, then he began to get involved with other owner/operators at the local co-op level. Soon, he picked up divisional responsibility and then became involved with the national MHOA organization before being elected its president.

"I think McDonald's has the right mindset when it comes to diversity," Hernandez says. "I've got whites, blacks, and Hispanics in all my stores as managers, and we are a team, and, without a doubt, we have an advantage over our competitors. These owner/operators wouldn't be where they are today, running their own million-dollar businesses, without McDonald's being fair."

Hispanic Business Vision

The effort to tie our diversity commitment to our business results intensified about five years ago when we began to work on our Hispanic Business Vision. This was a comprehensive look at all aspects of our business with the idea of making McDonald's the most widely used and respected company by the Hispanic community.

Creating the Hispanic Business Vision involved a crossfunctional team from all parts of the system, including franchisees, employees, and suppliers—Hispanic and non-Hispanic. We started with a recognition that the country was changing very fast, which meant that the insights we developed in looking at the entire McDonald's experience from an Hispanic point of view were valuable for looking at our business from other customer areas as well.

"We determined that the Hispanic Business Vision is not going to just be about Hispanics," Hernandez says. "It's about serving all of our customers. It has to be inclusive of everybody because we are all owner/operators who want to meet the needs of all of our customers."

Hernandez remembers that the process started slowly because they were moving into new territory, but it soon picked up momentum as they looked at every aspect of our business for all of our customers. "It was a great tool," he says. "We met with outside experts who understood the culture, and some of the leading people from the system were not even Hispanic."

This work is integral to the development of our business plans every year, leading our strategies with insights from our diverse base of customers.

People with Disabilities

At McDonald's, our commitment to provide work opportunities for people with disabilities extends back to the 1960s. In 1981, however, we stepped up our efforts in an organized way with the creation of the McJobs program, which is designed to help physically and mentally challenged individuals develop skills and confidence to succeed in the workplace environment of our restaurants.

Through McJobs, we recruited candidates by contacting state vocational rehabilitation (VR) agencies, which helped us establish partnerships with local agencies and schools. In turn, VR agencies referred candidates to us that they believed would benefit most.

Before the candidates even began training in our restaurants, our crew, managers, and area supervisors participated in a sensitivity training seminar. Part of the seminar included role-playing so our own people could understand that people with disabilities have the same wants and needs as anyone else.

When the candidates came into our restaurants, they trained shoulder-to-shoulder with a job coach for about eight weeks. In addition to the training, McJobs coaches followed up by conducting monthly network meetings to provide a social environment to discuss work-related concerns.

Win-Win Scenarios

There were a lot of winners when we combined our time-tested formula of top management support, training, and networking to the employment of people with disabilities.

Disabled employees were able to develop a professional, "can-do" attitude that comes with the territory at McDonald's. Crew members became more sensitive and aware. And managers and supervisors found that they were gaining loyal, dependable, and highly motivated employees.

Our spokesperson for the McJobs program was Chris Burke, a 25-year-old New Yorker with Down Syndrome, who starred in the ABC television series "Life Goes On."

And a young man born with Down Syndrome named Mike Sewell joined the crew of our restaurant in Carey, North Carolina in 1989 and became a celebrity in his own right when a commercial featuring him appeared during the Super Bowl in 1991. The inspiring commercial highlighted the importance of his job in his own life and won numerous awards for celebrating the ability of people with disabilities to succeed in the workplace.

As Ed Rensi said in a keynote address to the President's Committee on the Employment of Disabled People in May of 1990, "We know it's good business to recognize our disabled customers. But we think it's even better business to recognize people with disabilities as talented, committed, and productive employees."

Local Innovation

Helping people with disabilities succeed in their local restaurant jobs often prompted innovative solutions.

One such example came when Cary Marchand, manager of one of our restaurants in Columbia, Missouri hired Chris Carrawell to prepare salads under the McJobs program in 1991. Marchand commented at the time, "Chris had more enthusiasm than anyone I had ever seen."

Unfortunately, due to her disability, Carrawell had trouble remembering where all the salad ingredients needed to be placed, so she could only prepare 48 salads per day—less than half the amount the restaurant required.

So her job coach, Tracy Fetters, developed a salad template that Carrawell could place over each salad plate that indicated where each topping was to be placed.

"I was amazed when I saw the template because it made Chris's training so much easier, and the neatness and accuracy of each salad was impressive," Marchand said.

As a result, Carrawell was able to increase her output to 100 salads per day, showing how making adaptations brought out the ability of people with disabilities. Because of that success, the template also became standard practice for crew members in all our restaurants.

Leading the Law

Indeed, because of our early involvement in employing people with disabilities, when the employment phase of the Americans with Disabilities Act (ADA) took effect in July of 1992, it was essentially a nonevent for McDonald's.

We had not only supported enactment of the legislation, but we had also participated in advising lawmakers on how to make the new law effective and we were a source of information for many other companies who contacted us for advice.

As Rogercarole Rogers said at the time, "We will continue to accommodate employees with disabilities at all levels of the system—not just because it's the law, but because it's good business. Our focus is on people's abilities, not disabilities—and that's the way we should work with all our employees."

To help our restaurant owners and managers sort through the implications of the new law, we created yet another training seminar—"Employing People with Disabilities"—and made it available through regional Human Resources departments.

Those seminars focused on the law and its ramifications on our system; sensitivity training to the barriers faced by people with disabilities; the interviewing process, including appropriate questions to ask and interviewing etiquette; and reasonable tools we had adopted to accommodate various disabilities in the workplace.

Some examples of these accommodations included adjusting bells, buzzers, and timers on the fryers so that employees with visual impairments could know when products are ready; Braille labels on salad ingredients; and wheelchair access for drive-thru cashiers.

We continued to reach out to local agencies that served the disabled in their own communities to create relationships where they would refer qualified people and even provide job training assistance in some cases. Our experience showed us that the extra training effort in the beginning paid dividends over time, as our retention rates for people hired under the McJobs program was consistently in the upper 80 percent range.

And, as we have demonstrated throughout our diversity efforts, our determination to do the right thing paid off for the business as well.

As Rogers puts it, "When people with disabilities know that McDonald's is receptive to them—through our commercials, employment record, and the personal experiences they have— then people with disabilities feel that McDonald's is a place for them to go to. It's not the law that brings that quality to McDonald's—it's an attitude we already have, and we mean to keep it."

Employment opportunities for people with disabilities also apply to our home office employees as well, and they are valued equally with their counterparts in every area.

We've installed special phones that provide printed messages where appropriate, our elevators are clearly marked in Braille, and we offer sign language classes to employees. This demonstrates our belief that the only real disability is the loss of opportunity.

"McJobs" 20 Years Later

I find it ironic that the word "McJobs" created such a furor when the Merriam-Webster Dictionary included it in its 11th edition to describe "a low-paying job that requires little skill and provides little opportunity for advancement."

Our CEO at the time, the late Jim Cantalupo, was understandably angry and upset and wrote a letter to the editor of the dictionary saying that definition was not only inaccurate, but it was an insulting depiction of jobs at McDonald's. "Restaurant employees are proud of their jobs and recognize that restaurants are indeed gateways to opportunity, not to mention the paychecks they provide," Cantalupo wrote. "According to the National Restaurant Association, restaurants are the nation's largest private-sector employer, offering all kinds of positions in a variety of fields, providing quality jobs for nearly 9 percent of those employed in the United States for a year or a career."

Cantalupo's strong response prompted a nationwide discussion on the value of first jobs and the opportunities they provide. Even *The Wall Street Journal* weighed in with an editorial that said, in part:

> It helps to remember that the McDonald's employee demographic is a varied one: students working their way through school, immigrants getting their introduction to the U.S. labor force, seniors looking to keep busy, parents supplementing the family income, and even, yes, the occasional breadwinner down on his luck and looking for immediate cash. . . . And while we're on the subject, let's mention two other things that Mr. Cantalupo cites. First, that *Fortune* magazine designated the hamburger giant as America's best company for minorities. Second, McDonald's really has something it calls "McJobs": a 20-year-old program that trains the mentally and physically handicapped for jobs they otherwise might never get. Maybe it's time for the folks at Merriam-Webster to wake up and smell the fries.

I think the whole controversy shows that it sometimes takes factual background and historical perspective to understand an issue before printing a derisive definition.

Asian Americans

In more recent years, McDonald's has also formalized our diversity efforts for our Asian American employees and owner/operators, as they represent a rapidly growing demographic force in the country today.

Though fewer in number within McDonald's system than their Hispanic counterparts, our Asian American employees and owner/operators are similar in that they represent a multitude of different cultures and backgrounds. And as their numbers have increased in the system, so has their influence in helping us understand and cater to the diversity of interests among our Asian American customers.

Ted Tongson, who has since left the system, was our first Asian owner/operator when he opened a restaurant in Paris, Texas in 1975. Today, more than 70 Asian American franchisees own and operate some 350 restaurants across the system.

Victor Lim found opportunity with McDonald's in Hawaii in 1974. A native of Rangoon, Burma, his family left the country that was to become known as Myanmar after a military coup in 1963 and settled in Thailand after a short stay in Singapore. While earning his MBA at the University of Hawaii, he decided to practice interviewing before he graduated.

"McDonald's said they were willing to hire me right away and work around my school schedule," Lim recalls, "so I decided if the company was crazy enough to do that, I should give it a chance."

Lim never worked anywhere else, and in 1987, having risen to the head of operations for the Asia/Pacific region, he bought the restaurant where he had started as a trainee and today owns seven restaurants, all in Honolulu. Looking back, Lim likens his early days in the company as the "wild, wild west" for young minorities trying to get ahead.

"In those early days on the corporate side, I really feel that there were unnecessary and unseen roadblocks in people's way," Lim says. "Today, McDonald's management has a better grasp of what diversity is, recognizing the differences from one culture to the other."

Birth of the Network

During a tour of duty in Los Angeles, Lim planted the seeds for the Asian Employee Business Network, hosting a potluck dinner at his home for several of his fellow Asian employees who were working at the store level throughout Southern California. "I was the only Asian in mid-management at that time," Lim says. "Most of the people got stuck at the store manager level and very few moved beyond that. So our mission was to get people the right opportunity to show their abilities and talent and grow within the system."

One of the people who benefited from the Asian network was Karen Garcia, born in Baker, Montana after her American father met and married her Korean mother during the Korean War. She started as a high school crew member at a McDonald's restaurant in 1975 after the family moved to California.

"Coming from a very small town where we were the only Asian American family, I was very keenly aware that we were different," she says. "At McDonald's, I saw more people like me. Then, as my career grew, I was able to feel even more comfortable as I connected with the other women in McDonald's, as well as the other Asian employees."

Today, Garcia is a vice president in the Southern California Region and chair of the National Asian Employee Network. "The value of the network is creating opportunities for multiple Asian employees to get together and share similarities and to be able to work through some of the challenges and barriers based on our cultural upbringing," she says. "I think one of our greatest strengths, but also one of our barriers, is that we're extremely strong workers, but we don't always communicate upwards to our bosses."

Yet another challenge we face in recruiting strong Asian employees and owner/operators is the desire among many immigrant Asian families to have their children educated well enough to move into careers like law and medicine.

"He Hung Up on Me"

Glen Kikuchi, an owner/operator in the Baltimore/Washington Region, remembers when he called his father back in Hawaii in 1974 with the news that he was joining McDonald's after leaving the

Army as a captain. "My father was so ticked off, he hung up on me," Kikuchi recalls with a laugh. "I called him back a second time and said we must have been disconnected but I just wanted to tell him I was going to start working for McDonald's. And the phone went dead again. After I calmed him down, I explained all the possibilities and how I wanted to own my own business and that there were a lot of opportunities."

Kikuchi didn't see a lot of other Asians on the East Coast when he first began with McDonald's, but he was nevertheless impressed by the company's commitment to minorities. His regional manager, director of operations, area supervisor, and restaurant manager were all African Americans.

"My introduction to McDonald's included diversity from day one, although 'diversity' was not the term that was used back then," he says. "I could see that people of minority status were in positions of leadership, and the emphasis was always on performance. And because the system was growing so rapidly at the time, there were always promotional opportunities if you were ready, qualified, and aggressive enough to spend your own time learning the business."

Kikuchi fit that mold. Within 11 months he was a store manager and quickly advanced to area supervisor, field consultant, operations manager, and field services manager before moving to the home office as staff director of National Operations. Ultimately, he advanced to regional manager in Baltimore in 1989 before becoming an owner/operator in 1984.

– – – – – – –

Training Is Outstanding

"I have never really felt isolated because we have always had a network," Kikuchi says. "Today, it's more formalized and the training is outstanding, centering on individual development. Today, diversity is part of the McDonald's fabric, and I see that continuing because we have so much talent in the pipeline. Even if we wanted to, we could not stop the advancement of diversity that McDonald's has supported for so many years."

Kikuchi was interested in becoming a franchisee when he first arrived at McDonald's, and today he owns and operates 10 restaurants. "Well before he died, my father came to love McDonald's," Kikuchi says. "He loved the concept and he was very proud that I had achieved so much success."

"I Could Own Something"

Unlike many of his colleagues, Steven Eng left a successful outside career to join McDonald's as an owner/operator. Eng's family came from Hong Kong, where they owned a restaurant, to New York in 1964 when he was 11 years old. After high school, he enrolled in the hotel and hospitality program at Cornell University where he first heard about the McDonald's system during a school seminar.

"I thought it was a fabulous idea, a restaurant as part of a system, but after I graduated, I went for the high-profile, glamorous job while McDonald's stayed in the back of my mind," Eng recalls.

Many years later, after working for Hilton International, Bank of America, and American Express, Eng decided he wanted to be an entrepreneur. "I realized I could never own a bank, but, with McDonald's, I could own something for myself, be part of a big system, and be successful," he says. So he called McDonald's and purchased his first restaurant in the heart of San Francisco's Chinatown district, just a block and a half from where he lived.

"I didn't know much about diversity when I came to McDonald's," Eng recalls. "I wanted to be an operator first, I was looking for a company that cared about people and cared about operators, and I knew that I could be an asset for the company in Chinatown."

After establishing himself in the community—where Eng and his wife now own four restaurants in South San Francisco—he became involved with the Asian McDonald's Operator Association (AMOA) and ultimately rose to become its national president, helping to develop the Asian Business Vision.

"A key issue for us today is helping the system to understand more about this growing consumer base," Eng says. "Asians have great disposable purchasing power, they index higher than any other group, and they may be a small group but they're growing very fast. The Asian Business Vision is about the food we serve, the people we hire and being sensitive to our Asian consumers. It's also about the way we design our restaurants so that they're conducive to the nuances that are important to Asians, such as family values."

Lim notes that Asian operators helped establish the Asian Consumer Marketing (ACM) program at McDonald's in 2002—the first of its kind for the industry. "No other quick-service restaurant has a dedicated national budget and plan to address the ACM, and today, we do it as an everyday part of doing business," Lim says. "Everything we do with McDonald's national campaigns is very similar, yet everything has subtle differences and slightly different twists for individual markets and that's something I can take advantage of as an Asian operator."

The Asian Business Vision grew out of this increased attention to the ACM, and Garcia sees several advantages of tapping the expertise of Asian operators and employees in the way they can help all restaurants succeed.

"Our diversity helps our business because we're educating folks," Garcia says. "Most people would say that the Asian population is concentrated on the East and West Coast, but it's a lot more dispersed today than it ever has been. And advertising in the ACM also breaks down some of these myths that Asian employees are not going to come and work at McDonald's because it's not a medical or educational profession."

———————

Scholarship Program

Because Eng and his Asian colleagues recognize the importance of education to Asian families, the AMOA took the lead in establishing a national scholarship program. They worked with McDonald's and our partners at Coca-Cola to form the first national Asian scholarship fund, called Asian and Pacific Islander American Scholarship Fund. And our Asian operators are deeply involved in their own communities as well, through RMHC and their own charitable efforts.

Lim sums up the value of diversity to McDonald's this way: "The system today is more open to new approaches and different avenues. We are more receptive to the fact that America is made up of so many different colors.

"We used to create a stew of everything," he says, "but today it's more like a salad bowl. There are different ingredients, but they can be separate and still part of a bigger system."

———————

Gay and Lesbian Employees

A recent diversity group to emerge within McDonald's involves our gay and lesbian employees. This has been somewhat slow to emerge as a distinct community within the company because sexual preferences are typically a private concern, there are no physical characteristics that distinguish members of the group, and societal attitudes have been slow to change over the years.

One of the triggering events within McDonald's that allowed this to happen came in 2004, when the company enabled domestic partners to become eligible for our benefits package. When it was announced, it was a clear sign that the company officially recognized the legitimacy of same-sex partners and demonstrated the executive team's support of its gay and lesbian employees.

Once that was added to our benefits package, the pattern that worked for so many other groups began to establish itself. People began to meet informally in small groups to discuss common issues, these meetings grew in size and ultimately became the basis for the Gay and Lesbian Network, and now chapters are forming in regions all around the country.

Yet another triggering event was the arrival of Richard Ellis in 2005, an openly gay man in a long-time committed relationship, as the officer in charge of U.S. Communications. Ellis was no stranger to McDonald's, having held a similar position in Canada since 2000 and serving as a consultant to McDonald's at a Canadian public relations agency for 12 years prior to that.

His appointment was not only another clear signal of management's support of gay and lesbian employees, but our efforts above and beyond the call of duty cemented Ellis' belief of the company's commitment as well.

As Ellis recalls, "When I was asked to come from McDonald's Canada to run U.S. Communications, there were a lot of other people who could have taken on that role. It would have been a lot easier because U.S. management had to deal with immigration challenges to bring me in from Canada, and then they had to deal with same-sex immigration for my partner coming into the United States."

For Ellis, who is now Senior Vice President of Communications and Public Affairs, McDonald's Canada, it was a signal of management support that was just as clear as its approval of the domestic partner benefits package. "When you live and breathe McDonald's values in a real way that impacts your employees and their families and everybody else around them that they touch, that's inclusion. That's diversity in action."

Growing Network

I asked Ellis to be the officer lead for McDonald's Gay and Lesbian and Allies Network (MGLAN), and that truly triggered a response. Initially, most of the growth came in the home office, where there have traditionally been a number of gay and lesbian professional employees and it's easier for them to get to know one another. More recently, the network has been springing up in various regions around the country, including the Great Southern, Pacific Sierra, Pacific Northwest, New York, and Indianapolis regions. And now they have acquired sufficient critical mass and have held their first network symposium in mid 2009.

"We went to the 'Out and Equal' national conference two years in a row," Ellis says. "The first time we had 6 or 7 people from McDonald's and the next year we had 30, which is just one little microcosm that illustrates our growth. When we have a separate McDonald's Gay, Lesbian, and Allies Network Symposium of our own here in Chicago, that's going to be another of those watershed moments that's going to further grow the ranks of these groups."

Training Component

In addition to senior management support and our growing internal network, we also utilize our third important component to promote diversity—education and training. Our course is called "Sexual Orientation in the Workplace" and it has been run by a dynamic woman named Liz Winfeld.

I actually met her in 1999 when Raymond Mines, my executive officer at the time, delivered the keynote speech at a diversity conference in Hawaii. Attending one of the sessions at that conference, we were very impressed with Winfeld's dynamic presentation on maintaining a respectful workplace as it relates to gay, lesbian, bisexual, and transgender issues. I told her afterward that it was too early for us, but that I would call her when we were ready, and that's what I did after we passed the company's new benefits policy.

As Ellis notes, the training course is for straight individuals as well as gay and lesbian people. "It's about simple education, sensitivity awareness, establishing a respectful workplace, and promoting acceptance in the workplace," he says. "It's all the good things you would expect from a McDonald's training program and it's delivered with great energy."

The next challenge in extending our network is moving on to the restaurant level, where we clearly have a number of gay and lesbian employees we have been unable to reach. I believe, as Ellis does, that the fact that we have a growing number of people who deal directly with restaurants—like field service and operations consultants—now participating in the network in many regions could hasten the impact we have at the restaurant level.

And, like the rest of our diversity efforts, that ultimately translates into a positive impact on our business.

Direct Business Impact

"The power of the gay and lesbian dollar is huge," Ellis says. "Gays and lesbians tend to spend more of their disposable income on things like eating out, travel, entertainment, and clothes, and so there's a great fiscal opportunity to be able to penetrate the gay and lesbian market more specifically.

"At the same time, gay and lesbian consumers are very fickle. They watch very closely who they give their dollars to based on the kinds of societal changes they see. That's one of the reasons we have been one of the many sponsors of the San Francisco Gay Pride Parade, because it indicates McDonald's is a caring company as it relates to gay and lesbian employees and consumers."

Lessons Learned

One clear lesson that emerges from our experience in dealing with a multitude of diverse people within our organization is that not all groups are the same. That might seem obvious, but we had to overcome the tendency—especially in the early days—to view issues from the narrow focus of just two camps: white male managers and diversity groups.

It quickly becomes crystal clear that the issues that African Americans have are different from those of women, and they are both different from those of Hispanic Americans, and so on. Not only that, but some issues fade over time for each group and are replaced by others.

Sensitivity to the issues, attitudes, and behaviors that are different among diversity groups—and very often different within a single diversity group—is important if you are to recognize and manage those differences effectively.

Because of the cultural differences among our various diversity groups, for example, you will find a variety of responses to the same situation: ranging from outspoken anger, to quiet resentment, to inner hostility. All of these responses need to be understood and dealt with, not just the noisiest ones.

There is also a richness of diversity within each of these groups. Hispanic Americans, for example, are not a monolithic group by any means—it makes a significant difference if their heritage is Cuban, Mexican, Argentine, or any number of other subgroupings.

So, while we employ many of the same tools to help our diversity groups succeed within McDonald's, including training and networking, we work hard to tailor each of those techniques to the individuals we are helping. If you apply a cookie-cutter approach for all groups, you are in danger of tuning people out by not being sensitive to their unique needs.

One of the discoveries that has worked for McDonald's that I would recommend to those of you who are managing diversity within your organizations is making sure that your own department reflects the groups you are serving.

That's because a mixture of men and women from different ethnic backgrounds within your own department makes it much easier to relate to, and adapt to, the rich differences in your own workforce. A staff meeting will produce the same kinds of diverse ideas and opinions that you are working to create across your entire organization.

7

McDonald's Today

*M*el Hopson always said that his goal was to work himself out of a job, and, as his successor, I feel the same way. When Mel and I compare notes today, it is clear that I am much closer to reaching that goal than he was when he retired because we have made some incredible strides in the evolution of diversity within McDonald's.

There is no question that we still have a number of challenges to meet and that there are ample opportunities for us to improve. However, we are much closer to institutionalizing inclusion and diversity as a way of life at McDonald's than we were 30 years ago.

When diversity simply becomes part of McDonald's culture—when everybody feels welcome and included and respected as partners within the business enterprise as a matter of course, when diversity becomes part of the very fabric of McDonald's—that's when the company will no longer need a separate department for inclusion and diversity.

The arrival of that day might have been hard to imagine when Mel was a full-time "tree shaker," but today, as our activities have become more like "jelly makers," it is easier to envision the time when our job here will be finished.

And a big reason for that is we continue to execute those things that worked so well in getting us to this point—training, networks, and top management support. As we've seen throughout our evolution of diversity, those are the elements that make a real difference in bringing diversity to life. In addition, the "secret sauce" in our approach is the fact that we have never stopped doing those things—our commitment to diversity is an all-the-time best effort.

Four Distinct Stages

Because of our consistent and constant approach, we have progressed through four stages of development at McDonald's.

The first was the affirmative action stage. In the beginning, we needed to emphasize equality of opportunity and provide remedies for past wrongs, whether intentional or accidental.

The primary measure of success in this initial stage of development was quantitative. In other words, the question we asked ourselves was, do we have enough African Americans, and women, and Hispanics, and Asians, and Gays and Lesbians yet?

The next stage was recognizing differences.

Once we created a more diverse team of people, we worked to acknowledge the unique differences among our colleagues so that we could support their individual contributions to our business.

The question at this stage was, are we sharing with each other and listening to new ideas yet?

The next step was valuing differences.

The focus of this stage of development was creating an environment where everyone felt included as part of the team and valued for the ideas and experiences and perspectives that they brought to the McDonald's system, thanks to their diverse backgrounds.

The measure of success in this stage is more qualitative, as in, do we all understand and respect each other yet?

And the fourth and final stage, which we are working to achieve today, is managing diversity.

This means using your diverse workforce as a strategic business tool to create competitive advantages or to solve specific business problems.

At this point, the question we are asking ourselves is, are we achieving the results we need yet?

Managing diversity means operating in a corporate culture where different views, opinions, experiences, educations, religions, and lifestyles are respected, where everyone is a valued and contributing member of the team, and where our actions are led by insights that create success in our business.

And that's where our responsibility is focused today, particularly in the U.S. business. We are helping all the organizations to live and breathe in an atmosphere where we are embracing diversity to achieve results and where diversity is part of every strategic business plan.

This progression is much clearer in hindsight than it was at the time we were fighting many of the initial battles. As Hopson says, "We didn't lay out this big master plan; it just evolved in terms of how we were doing things. And it worked!"

Small but Dedicated Staff

I have been blessed with a staff of people who are as committed to the principles of inclusion and diversity as I am. Though we are small in number, we accomplish a great deal because of the broad commitment of leaders throughout the system.

They include Kevin Bradley, of Chinese and Irish descent born and raised in Chicago; Gus Viano, a Hispanic born and raised in Argentina; and Lynda DuBovi, an Anglo-Saxon native of Chicago. Together, we are focused on incorporating inclusion and diversity principles into our talent management system so that they are embedded in the values and competencies that are part of our leadership culture. The mindset is already well established with the foundation we have laid within McDonald's.

Training

Another part of our job is helping coordinate the continuation of our curriculum of classes, workshops, and seminars that help employees understand what to do to succeed as we bring diversity to life in the organization and help our managers understand how to manage a diverse workforce.

The content of these courses has evolved as our own understanding of the issues important to everyone at McDonald's has developed and also as societal attitudes have shifted, both inside and outside the company. Nonetheless, the fundamentals of educating our people will always be a foundation of our approach to diversity.

Today, the courses we offer include Winning with Inclusion and Diversity, GenderSpeak, Asian Career Development, Black Career Development, Hispanic Career Development, Women: Enhancing Personal and Professional Effectiveness, Sexual Orientation in the Workplace, and Diversity and Inclusion from a White Male Perspective.

Employee Business Networks

We also act as advisors and consultants to our employee business networks, which have continued to grow and thrive through the years. All of them have active national organizations, and most have local chapters that bring together employees from throughout our system.

These include our Women's Leadership Network, our National Asian Employee Business Network, McDonald's African American Council, our Hispanic Employee Network, our McDonald's Gay, Lesbian and Allies Network, our Young Professionals Network, and our Working Mothers' Council. In addition to our own staff people assigned to assist each of the networks, we also have a company officer who works with each group and an executive sponsor who maintains leadership responsibility to keep our networks moving forward.

Because we support these networks, we enable people to be proud of who they are and to celebrate their diversity.

"Today, in large part because of the networks, people are able to come to work with their ethnicity," Viano says. "It's up to the company to use it or to lose it, and I have to say that McDonald's uses it very well."

Bradley, who works with some of the groups that are smaller in number, like our Asian and gay and lesbian employees, says that they are generally quieter but beginning to emerge.

"Our Asian symposium this year was about promoting yourself," he says. "In America, they say that the squeaky wheel gets the grease, where in Asia, the saying is the nail that sticks up the highest gets hit the hardest. And the gay and lesbian group has gone from the point of being afraid to having an e-mail distribution list to now having advertised meetings and achieving critical mass so they can have their own symposium."

Franchisee Networks

Our restaurant owner/operator networks, which played such important roles in prompting our initial diversity efforts, have grown into active, vibrant organizations that are largely self-sustaining today.

These include the National Black McDonald's Operators Association, McDonald's Hispanic Operators Association, the Asian McDonald's Operator Association, and the Women Operators Network. We work as liaisons with these groups as well, helping to facilitate the flow of information between them and our company people.

Both our employee and franchisee networks sponsor National Symposiums on a regular basis, as well as frequent conferences and seminars in the local regions, often combining forces on topics relevant both to employees and to owner/operators.

One of the unique aspects of our function is that we touch so many other areas as it relates to diversity. It's not just Corporate Human Resources; we touch supplier diversity, franchising, communication, supply chain, business units, and everyone else throughout the organization, including our liaison with our franchisees.

That's why we say that diversity is everybody's business at McDonald's. We are the catalysts that get things started—our managers and leaders provide the day-to-day energy that drives the diversity aspect of our business.

And each of us in the Inclusion and Diversity Department is also involved in our external partnerships, leading the relationships for each of our diverse groups throughout the United States, whether it's the NAACP and the National Urban League, La Raza and MALDEF, the Women's Foodservice Forum and Catalyst, Out and Equal, the Organization of Chinese Americans, or the President's Committee on Employment with People of Disabilities.

I wanted to mention our involvement in one organization in particular—the Multicultural Foodservice & Hospitality Alliance (MFHA)—because we participated as a founding partner in 1996, when its president, Gerry Fernandez, created the organization. We felt that MFHA's mission to promote the business case for inclusion and diversity in the foodservice and hospitality industry was completely aligned with our own vision. We have been active MFHA members ourselves, and I was honored to serve as the chair of its board of directors in 2004.

Leadership Commitment

The final component that has driven the evolution of diversity at McDonald's—leadership commitment—has taken an interesting turn in recent years. That's because a significant number of McDonald's senior management do more than support diversity—they represent a diverse group of leaders within their own ranks.

This came about as a result of the inevitable benefits that come to organizations that take a positive approach to diversity. As you open your doors to more and more people who weren't previously included, you deepen the talent pool. As the pipeline fills and the talent rises to the top, you will find that the best people reflect the diversity that you have created within the ranks of the company.

In other words, our senior leaders today were not picked because of their ethnic background or gender; they were chosen for the top positions because they were the best people for the job, regardless of their ethnic background or gender. We are blessed with a wider assortment of talented people to choose from because of our past efforts.

So I thought the best way to share this with you would be to bring you some of their stories and insights from their own experiences.

Hispanic Recruiting

Ralph Alvarez, McDonald's president and chief operating officer, tried to join McDonald's a couple of times early in his career and ultimately came on board in 1994 when we consciously began to recruit Hispanic leadership talent.

Born in Havana, Cuba, Alvarez came to the United States in 1960 at the age of five after Fidel Castro took over the Cuban government. His family didn't consider themselves immigrants at that time. "We left thinking it would be a short stay and then we'd go back, but we never have," he says.

After graduating from the University of Miami in three years, Alvarez went to work with a large accounting firm and then joined one of his clients—Burger King, headquartered in Miami. Alvarez wound up working in Madrid, London, and Toronto—experiences that helped him decide that McDonald's was the place to be in the industry.

"I tried getting into McDonald's in 1987 and again in 1989, but couldn't get in the door," Alvarez says. "I was told they mostly hired from within, so I went to work for Wendy's for the next four years.

Then McDonald's called me, and the beauty of that call was that they had identified a need for Hispanic leadership and were recruiting talent. The rest, to me, has been the opportunity to succeed, based on my skills, and not necessarily because of my heritage or my native language."

Along the way, Alvarez has served as president of McDonald's Mexico, a U.S. division president, and president of the U.S. company before taking the number two position in the company and joining the Board of Directors in 2008. And to him, the secret to diversity is continuous improvement.

"This is not one of those things where there's an end game and you get there and then you're done," he says. "These are societal issues that go back generations—they don't change in one generation. Success has to mean that you're as comfortable in the environment where you work as you are at home, and that people value your differences, your creativity, and your performance."

What Alvarez values most today is the business success that McDonald's enjoys with its diverse executive team. "There's a stereotype out there that says you can do this diversity thing and get people into slots, but then you're not going to be as good," Alvarez says. "Instead, we have people in positions throughout our company because they are talented first. Our business is thriving. That, to me, says it all."

Engineering a Career

Don Thompson, who today is our highest ranking African American executive as president of McDonald's USA, took a different route, rising through the ranks from his original position as an engineer.

Born in Chicago, Thompson moved to Indianapolis, Indiana at the age of 10, attended local schools, and then graduated from Purdue University with a degree in electrical engineering. He was working for a defense contractor who made radar-jamming programs in the late 1980s when he got his first call from a recruiter, who he turned down flat.

"I was told the job involved robotics and control circuitry, which sounded rather interesting," Thompson recalls with a laugh. "I thought that the job was with McDonnell Douglas, but when the recruiter said that it was McDonald's, the hamburger company, I told them they had the wrong guy."

A second call revealed that McDonald's was looking to broaden its diversity efforts, and Thompson began to appreciate the broad nature of the business and the possible opportunities. "There were a number of small things I liked as well, such as McDonald's involvement in community activities, so I decided to give it a try," he says.

He began as an engineer in the restaurant equipment area, and credits the Black Career Development course with opening his eyes about issues that affect minorities in large companies.

"The course itself was very revealing in terms of pushing buttons on how we viewed McDonald's and being aware of how some people might be acting out toward us," Thompson remembers. "It was a good chance to meet people who had some of the same issues and to speak frankly with them, and also a good orientation process into the business itself. I also met a broad network of African Americans throughout other parts of the company and became a part of that network."

Early in his career, Thompson was getting frustrated and was thinking about leaving McDonald's. At that point, Mel Hopson and I asked him to sit down with Raymond Mines, one of our senior African American officers, and have a discussion before he made a final decision. Today, Thompson credits that with turning his career around, although it took some time to play out.

"Raymond was a very gruff guy, and when I told him that I wanted to have an impact on the business, he suggested I go to work for another department and earn a promotion to director," Thompson says. "He said, 'who knows, some day you might come to work for me,' which I thought was kind of arrogant at the time, but as it turns out, he was my mentor ever after that and, unbeknownst to me, he became my executive sponsor."

As Thompson moved into the operations part of McDonald's, he proved himself in a number of situations, as a regional manager, president of the Western Division of the U.S. business, and chief operations officer of McDonald's USA. He was elevated to his current position of president of McDonald's USA in August of 2006, and he credits our increased diversity for much of the success we've enjoyed in the marketplace over the past four to five years.

Leveraging Diversity

"We have moved along a continuum of diversity from talking about it and acknowledging it and, today, are on the cusp of leveraging diversity to be so much better," he says. "Because our management team is so diverse, we are sensitive to how important diversity is. We've engrained procedures, we constantly talk about who's in the pipeline, and our owner/operators and their networks help keep us focused. We're really much better at diversity today—but I will add quickly that we still have a way to go to get where we want to be."

Thompson points out that the U.S. business plan is led with insights from minority groups—from music to food flavors to more energetic and active ways of marketing our products. Many of the changes that we've made in our menu have been led by the women in the organization, according to Thompson.

"We continue to realize that what we do with the diversity of our multicultural environment is a 'green' decision, because it's good for the business," Thompson says. "Going forward, we have to make sure that the pipeline is diverse and continues to be that way. We can't be satisfied by a false sense of security from the figureheads that we have today, so we have to keep the pipeline strong."

Feeding the Pipeline

Steve Russell, Senior Vice President and Chief People Officer for our U.S. business, is probably the one person who is most responsible for the care and feeding of our pipeline in the U.S. And, since HR has always been our greatest champion of inclusion and diversity, Russell and his team continue to provide strong support for our efforts.

When Russell joined McDonald's from Ameritech in 1996, he was able to look at our diversity efforts with the fresh eyes of an outsider. "I was blown away because McDonald's was like nothing I'd ever seen in terms of diversity," Russell remembers. "The culture of McDonald's is continuous improvement; it's one of our core values. I've never known a company that is so focused on always getting better, never getting complacent, and never accepting the status quo."

Russell believes that diversity will be a key differentiator between McDonald's and other companies we compete with for employees in the future.

"We're a company that promotes from within," Russell says. "The vast majority of our officers come from within the company, so we are doing much better at creating a diverse feeder pool by improving the diversity within our middle ranks, which then makes it easier to improve the diversity of our senior ranks.

"My job is to ensure that we keep that culture and continually improve it so that our employees can leverage and utilize this wonderful infrastructure that's already been built."

Started As Crew

The second-highest ranking officer in our U.S. business is Jan Fields, chief operations officer, who started almost by accident at McDonald's as a crew member in one of our restaurants in 1977.

"I was actually on my way to an interview for an 8 to 5 job in Dayton, Ohio, and stopped at a McDonald's to have a Coke," Fields recalls. "I saw a sign that said, 'Now Hiring—Flexible Hours,' so I asked the manager what that meant and he said that it was anything I wanted it to be, so I applied and he hired me."

Fields remembers that most of the employees then were white males, but that didn't particularly bother her, since she grew up with five brothers. She advanced to restaurant manager in short order, and remembers that the environment for women at McDonald's actually seemed to get worse once the Women in the Workforce classes began.

"I actually thought people were being mean to me because I was beating them with record sales and profits, but after a while I realized they were afraid women were going to pass them up," Fields says. "When the classes started, it was no longer about me, it was about this force that was developing and a genuine fear of women in the workplace."

Fields credits a zero-tolerance policy by McDonald's leadership for turning things around, along with placing role models in key positions, such as Raymond Mines as regional manager in Ohio.

"Raymond was very much of the new school, and it was a culture shift that was unbelievable," she says. "So many times in those early years I was going to leave, but Raymond was why I stayed. Little by little, people started recognizing the power of diversity and the power of putting people in places where they flourish.

"In my career, I've found that people of diverse backgrounds, particularlly those who have faced challenges—be they white, black, Hispanic, or whatever—typically worked harder because of where they came from. So we opened up our world and it was good for our business."

Like most of McDonald's leaders, Fields herself took advantage of the opportunities afforded by this evolving environment by serving as regional manager and president of one of our U.S. divisions before being elevated to her current position. And she recognizes the continuing challenge of taking diversity to another level.

"First of all, we're proud of where we are today; I don't think anybody would argue that," she says. "But we can never be satisfied, because that's not our culture. We can get better in how we truly give confidence to people at an even greater level—not just put them in a job, but get them ready to go into jobs and give them a higher level of confidence.

"You risk losing some people along the way because the truth is, if you get people who are really good and then they don't get what they're ready for, they leave. Actually, I'm always happy when someone can go and make him or herself better. They're not leaving because they don't want to be at McDonald's; they're leaving because they got an even better opportunity."

Fields also believes that maintaining what we do in terms of training and networking will always be the basis of our commitment to diversity, even though the specifics of the programs might change as our environment continues to change.

"There are a lot of women in different jobs now, but the workshops and the networks still serve a purpose," Fields says. "At some point, the purpose will be different. It will be because the participants like to be together and they want to do things together. It's not going to be because they had to do it to get equal education or because it was an early chance to learn."

Startling Complexion Change

The niche that Gloria Santona stepped into at McDonald's when she was hired fresh out of the University of Michigan Law School by our Legal department in 1977 was already unique from a diversity standpoint. In fact, she was hired by Noel Kaplan, the same man who hired me.

"Our Legal department had 13 lawyers at the time," Santona says. "There was one African American male, an Asian female, a Hispanic male, and me. That was pretty amazing in those days, but I didn't sense it was unusual for McDonald's."

Santona, who has since risen to become one of the few female Hispanic Corporate Counsels in the United States, discovered that the path to the top was not so rapid for women in the operations and management areas of the company. She recalls how we had one female assistant vice president, the lowest level officer you could be, as the role model to look up to for some 15 years.

"It's almost startling how the complexion of the company has changed over time," Santona says. "I see so many women now in the U.S. business, an absolutely amazing number, who are officers. And now the whole racial and ethnic diversity is here. Once you develop critical mass, things escalate. The pipeline is pretty robust, and that makes diversity something that's going to be sustainable— it's not a blip in history."

Building the Church

So, as we continue to manage the evolution of diversity at McDonald's, we keep in mind that we're working hard to work ourselves out of a job. It's like we've finished with the missionary work, we have plenty of converts to the religion, and now we're busy building the church so the congregation can take over.

But we not only still have a lot of work to do to make sure we continue building on the solid foundation we've laid for that church in the United States, we also are bringing McDonald's diversity to our partners around the world.

And that's our biggest challenge as we look forward to the next chapter of diversity at McDonald's.

Lessons Learned

What makes the difference between a successfully diversified organization and one that is not?

I believe the answer is persistence. Reggie Webb, who has been one of our long-time leaders in demonstrating the value of diversity, says it this way—"The main thing is to keep the main thing the main thing." That's a powerful thought expressed in a few simple words.

To put it another way, diversity within your organization is not a destination you will ever reach; it is a journey you decide to take. The decision to establish an effective diversity initiative should not have a numeric goal where you can say, "Okay, we're done now—it's time for something else." While it is important to establish milestones, you should be making a conscious decision to create a culture that embraces diversity every day, all the time.

As we have seen in these pages, McDonald's has approached diversity through management commitment, training and education, and networking. These are each important tools and techniques I would recommend to everyone.

But the real secret of our success has been the constant application of these important principles in good times and bad, no matter what swings we have experienced in the business cycle.

And that is the advice I would share with any other organization seeking to establish a diversity-rich culture: Stay with it! The moment you feel as if you've arrived and decide to cut back on your efforts is the moment that you will regress. Halting your efforts because of a business slowdown puts you back at square one—it not only sends a short-term message that you don't value diversity, but it also hurts your business in the long run.

The decision to embrace diversity is just as important as other business decisions your organization makes, like being the low-cost producer or the most consumer friendly. You need to stay as true to your commitment to diversity as you do to these other principles, because if you don't, you will suddenly find yourselves falling behind.

The key lesson is that diversity is not something you do—it's who you are.

8

Tomorrow . . . the World!

$\mathcal{O}$ ver the past couple of years, an increasingly large amount of my time has been devoted to taking the best practices that we've learned about the benefits of inclusion and diversity in the United States and sharing them with our partners in markets around the world. While the principles remain the same, the challenges are more varied because of the different cultural and societal issues that exist throughout the 118 countries where we do business outside of the United States.

On the business side, McDonald's has been phenomenally successful in spreading a U.S. concept to many different markets around the world. That's been due in large part to our de-centralized approach to managing our business. Many people are surprised to learn that we have fewer than 50 Americans residing overseas to help run our businesses. Instead, we purposely find local management people in the countries where we operate.

Local management, owner/operators, restaurant workers, and suppliers give us the ability to adapt the McDonald's system to the cultures and customs of our customers. We describe this approach as "glocal"—we are global in scope, but local in execution. In that sense, we have embraced diversity in our approach to our international business from the very beginning.

There are many examples that illustrate how we adapt to our individual markets. While our menu features all the McDonald's familiar favorites in every market—from burgers to fries to soft drinks—there is room for individuality to meet local tastes. So we serve lamb instead of beef in India, we feature kosher food in Israel, a Halal menu in the Middle East, beer in Germany, and so on. In Japan, Ronald McDonald was even renamed "Donald" McDonald by our local partner so Japanese people could pronounce his name more readily.

Our marketing is also adapted to our local markets under the global theme of "i'm lovin' it." While the theme remains the same around the world, each country has the freedom within that framework to execute marketing programs that are relevant and meaningful to local customers.

Local Diversity

In that context, our diversity efforts on a global basis must be a great deal more nuanced than a one-size-fits-all initiative.

Just as each country adapts the McDonald's system in ways that have an impact within their own borders, so too will our diversity approach vary to meet the individual needs of a particular country.

As our General Counsel Gloria Santona points out, our global efforts will push the comfort zone for some people, so we will have to be careful and sensitive not to push things too far too fast.

"Clearly, companies that are global like McDonald's have not quite figured out the future yet," Santona says. "I don't know that anybody has. The issue of diversity is complicated when you get outside the United States and you have to translate all the cultures and history and try to get to a place that's comfortable.

"Everybody needs to be a little uncomfortable, but if you get too uncomfortable you get turned off. It's a question of trying to find that delicate balance where you respect individual cultures and individual histories, and yet try to promote the principles and the values that you believe are right."

Maura Havenga, senior vice president of Worldwide Operations & Systems in our Restaurant Solutions Group, sees those same complexities in the countries she visits as part of her operational duties.

"Each area of the world has their own diversity challenges," Havenga says. "It's this diversity within diversity that's extremely challenging. But what's happening in each area of the world with their own cultures is reflected in the world of McDonald's when it comes to people, opportunity, and growth."

And that means the leaders of McDonald's business in each of those countries will be the diversity leaders for their organizations, because they understand better than anyone what's necessary to make our business stronger in their companies.

The Principles Are Important

Rich Floersch, our executive vice president and chief human resources officer, points out that it's the principles that are important.

"The whole beauty of this thing is not that we're taking a U.S. program and saying that you must be part of it," Floersch says. "We're saying that you can take these principles—not programs and practices, but principles—and apply them in our international markets with the appropriate amount of customization.

"Our success has been directly attributed to this locally relevant strategy. That's where I think we will be able to really benefit over time, with the greater diversity we see and a stronger pipeline of talent that we can have in some of our markets."

Two-Way Street

Ralph Alvarez, president and chief operating officer, sees the relationship between the company and our international employees as a two-way street.

"Our employees come to work for an American company, they love us for being a cultural brand, and we need to adapt culturally," Alvarez says. "But folks who work for us in those situations have a better understanding of American culture, and we do a lot of joint training together. They understand that diversity is part of our culture and those company values are not in conflict with the values of the counties where we operate.

"We're not out there to change the world; that's not our role. But we can plant a seed where that starts happening, and the world becomes a smaller place."

Havenga adds that the consumer-driven model that governs our business and the diversity framework of leadership commitment, training, and networking that we've developed in the United States means that the McDonald's business model can work in other countries as well.

"It's a very fluid model that's not set in stone," Havenga says. "It has a lot of flexibility in it, it has evolved over the years, and its foundation, I believe, is based upon the consumer."

Starting With Gender

As we look at the various countries we serve around the world, it's clear that diversity can be extremely complex, difficult to define, and different from country to country. But the one common issue that cuts across every country where we operate is gender. So we decided that was where we would start, because equal opportunity among men and women is a universal challenge.

And, even though we have just recently begun our efforts in earnest, the first prerequisite for success—top management leadership support—has already been accomplished. This concept has not just been embraced by Jim Skinner, our CEO, and global leaders like Alvarez and Floersch, but also by the senior executives for each area of the world, including Don Thompson in the U.S., Denis Hennequin in Europe, Jose Armario for Canada and Latin America, and Tim Fenton in Asia/Pacific, Middle East and Africa (APMEA).

Thanks to their leadership, women within the McDonald's system feel comfortable forming networks of their own and beginning to deal with issues that affect them and their ability to reach their potentials in their careers. We've already formed a Women's Leadership Network in Europe and held our first meeting in the fall of 2007, and we are doing the same in Asia, where we held our first women's network meeting in 2008.

Once again, I have to give a lot of credit to my partners in Human Resources—in this case, led by our senior vice president of international HR, Don Crosby, who has done a lot of work paving the way for our diversity initiatives. I arrived in Japan in the middle of 2007, for example, to meet with Eikoh Harada, the CEO of our Japanese business, to talk about our women's initiative. Harada-san's first words were, "Don's been here, I've already started."

That would have been unheard of five years ago, according to Crosby. "The former leadership in Japan would not even entertain the subject or talk about females filling jobs in mid-management," Crosby says. "But Harada-san has a Western education and worked for other U.S.-based companies before McDonald's, so he understands the benefits of having more females in leadership positions and he's been actively behind it."

Ironically, both Fenton and Crosby started their McDonald's careers in the same region in upstate New York, the Albany Region—Fenton as a high school crew person in 1973 and Crosby in 1975 as a management trainee after serving in the Marines. Albany was one of the first regions where we initiated our women's diversity classes because it represented one of our biggest challenges.

"Albany had this reputation as a male-dominated, chauvinistic region," Fenton says with a laugh. "Our logo was a pirate with a spatula in his mouth—how much more male dominated could you be? I would personally give us a failing grade in diversity at that point, but at least we were talking about it."

Crosby calls Mel Hopson the "hero" of diversity because he came into the regions and shook things up. "At first I thought Mel was a little radical because he had a way of almost starting riots when he wanted to," Crosby says, "but he was really just talking about some common sense things. That was a good thing, because people needed to wake up and start thinking."

Fenton says that the push forward within the corporation first came on strong in the 1990s, after the foundation had been laid during the 1970s and 1980s.

"That's when we realized there is a business case for diversity," Fenton says. "It became clear that staffing for your crew in your restaurants should reflect the environment and the neighborhood in which you're doing business. That's when we got beyond lip service and on to the business case, and, to be honest, the benefits and results of diversity are undeniable."

Fenton had considerable experience in international markets, having opened Poland and worked in several Eastern European and Middle Eastern countries before he took on his latest role leading all of Asia/Pacific, the Middle East, and Africa, which include some of the most male-dominated countries in the world. Thanks to his leadership, we are already seeing progress in many countries across that area of the world.

"We recognize that there are challenges, but they are surmountable," Fenton says. "I am a capitalist, so I wouldn't make this commitment if I didn't think it would help the business. Talent should rise to the top—that's the way it works—and we have some very talented people.

"In a system like McDonald's, you take the best practices—like the networks—you scale them up, and you execute to the max. That's how we have gone from nothing two years ago to where we are today—it's scaling best practices, not the best programs."

Europe's "Mixed Bag"

Today, Europe is a "mixed bag" of cultures, with very different sensitivities and customs, according to Hennequin, who describes

McDonald's as more of a "melting pot" than any other company doing business in Europe.

"You have to look at Europe on a country-by-country basis," he says. "Switzerland, for example, is a very protective country that is hard on immigrants. France, on the other hand, with its colonial history, has about six million citizens that are Arabic or African by background."

Hennequin, a lawyer trained in economics, started his McDonald's career in 1984 in the restaurants as a management trainee. He rose to become president of McDonald's France and was named president of McDonald's Europe in 2005. Early in his career he made it a point to become personally involved in recruiting women to become franchisees in France. "The staff side was well represented by women, but we had no women owner/operators," he recalls. "I made it a point to meet with each applicant and brought in the first women as franchisees."

One of the challenges he hopes to overcome through the introduction of a Women's Leadership Network in Europe is the current gap in the pipeline between women working in our restaurants and those in supervisory positions. "We have more women store managers than men, but we are behind in the number of women pursuing operations careers," he says.

"The Women's Leadership Network is a different experience for many, and some felt uncomfortable at first. But I am sponsoring it because this shows that it is something that is okay to do, and now most women understand its purpose."

Hennequin's goal over the next decade is to have as many women as men in positions as Managing Directors of European countries. "We should have a balance of men and women that embraces all facets of our business," Hennequin says. "More diversity gives you a different perspective on our business, a different wealth of ideas. It's all about talent management, because ability comes first, but diversity means understanding that people are coming from different cultures, and they each add value to the corporation."

Latin America Evolving

In the traditionally macho Latin American cultures, the role of women in the workplace has been evolving as well, according to Armario, who came to the United States from Cuba as a youngster in 1961.

"Our restaurant managers were fewer than 25 percent women 10 years ago, and, today, more than half are women," Armario says. "You still see the glass ceiling in many cases, but some of it is self-imposed because, in some markets, women are still the mother figure in the traditional sense and, even though they may have a career, they will say, 'Enough. This is as far as I want to go.'"

Training and education are critically important in making diversity successful, according to Armario, because they prepare people for challenges.

"You have to be sure you can educate and give the right level of knowledge and experience to folks so that, when they get to those positions of greater responsibility and leadership, they will be successful," Armario says.

Armario believes that the expansion of diversity principles to other countries around the world has a bright future because it is part of the company's value system.

"A strength of the McDonald's culture is we are so embedded in our values, diversity being one of them, that if you come into the organization and you don't share those values, it becomes pretty obvious right away. So you've got to either get on the bandwagon or get out."

Diversity of Experience

As we take diversity global, we also open up McDonald's to yet another opportunity, and that is helping our people expand their thinking across country borders by providing a diversity of experiences for them, according to Floersch.

"We have a strong bias toward local nationals running our markets," Floersch says. "But there's an opportunity for us to have a much stronger diversity of experience in our population, and that means much more openness to crossfunctional and cross-geographic moves.

"That, to me, would be the kind of next generation of diversity—diversity of background or experience. You wind up with stronger alternatives and options when you've had multiple reference points to draw upon."

A Broader Focus

Our initial global experience has prompted McDonald's to once again expand our focus on how we transform our workplace into one that embraces diversity.

As we expanded into other countries, it quickly became obvious to us that, within a global system embedded in a global economy, we needed to extend our thinking beyond American laws and historical templates. Our challenge is to transform our thinking about diversity to the broader realm of intercultural outreach and inclusion.

Thus, we signal the continuation of our evolution with a new name for our department that reflects our wider focus: Global Inclusion and Intercultural Management. Just as our department name has evolved over time—from equal opportunity to affirmative action to diversity to inclusion and diversity—it is now time to reflect our identity for the twenty-first century.

The Next Step

Transforming lives has always been an important part of our mission. Continuing that mission globally through outreach, inclusion, and education is the next step in our evolution. Our newly named department will function as a service center that fosters inclusive practices, develops intercultural competence, and maintains an early warning system for McDonald's when demographic shifts, system stress, or legislative change might threaten our well-being.

Our vision continues to be that people within McDonald's global system will be able to fully achieve their potential in their work and in their lives.

That means we must create the environment and opportunity for everyone to contribute their best efforts and cultivate relationships that enhance trust.

Another Chapter

The results of going global—the latest chapter in the story of the evolution of diversity at McDonald's—are yet to be told.

If we have learned anything through our experiences, it is that instilling the principles of diversity and inclusion takes patience and persistence. I am confident that our model of leadership support, training and education, and networks will be able to spark the seeds of opportunity to benefit our people and our business everywhere we operate.

That's why I felt it was so important to write this book about how diversity has evolved at McDonald's and that's why I am so appreciative that you have spent the time to learn more about our story.

Lessons Learned

There are no competitive secrets here—I invite anybody working in a company, or with an association, institution, or organization, to steal our ideas on diversity and inclusion shamelessly. You are welcome to them because I believe the more we can embrace diversity and provide opportunities to others, the stronger our society and our world will be. Helping just one person reach their career potential helps all of us.

Embracing the principles of diversity and inclusion can be very difficult. It requires that people open their hearts and minds to new ideas and concepts. The effort, however, no matter how hard, is well worth it—it is a journey I recommend to all of you.

As Lee Dunham, the African American owner/operator who opened our very first New York restaurant, says, "If we can stay united and head in the same direction, everybody is represented and valued and can sit at the table and make a contribution. We can't lose with that—that's why we're going to be winners and that's why we're going to continue to grow."

So I can think of no better way to close this book than to repeat the wisdom that McDonald's Founder Ray Kroc used to say so often when McDonald's people were first learning to work together to make this company what it is today:

"None of us is as good as all of us."

A Note from the Author

One of McDonald's enduring values—a core principal that started with our founder, Ray Kroc—has been to give back to those who have contributed to our success. The last of 11 children, growing up in a small, rural area in South Carolina, I never dreamed I would be given so many wonderful opportunities in my lifetime. Being able to write about the people who made these opportunities possible is one small way that I can give credit back to them. It is testimony to the fact that no one journeys through their lifetime alone.

This book is truly an expression of my appreciation to a company that has made it possible for me to achieve my potential as a person. I felt it was important to tell McDonald's remarkable story because there are so many others who can benefit and profit from our experience. I hope that as you have read through these pages, you feel the same inspiration and enthusiasm as I do for the ability of individual people to make a difference—a difference in crafting your own careers, in helping transform your companies and your communities, and in working to create a better society.

From the outset of this project, I felt strongly that the profits from the sale of this book should be donated to Ronald McDonald House Charities (RMHC), so we can continue to give back to families in need. That's why I am so proud that this book will not only share the remarkable story of the evolution of inclusion and diversity at McDonald's, but it will also contribute to the well being of children and families in our communities.

We founded RMHC 35 years ago in the memory of Ray Kroc, who died in 1984, and it has since grown into an expression of McDonald's commitment to children around the world.

Who knows which children today, no matter how humble their circumstances or what challenges they have to overcome, will grow up to become leaders in our society tomorrow, with a little help from us?

I thank all of you who have purchased this book. In doing so, you have contributed to making a meaningful impact on the lives of families in need. None of us is as good as all of us.

—Pat Harris

ACKNOWLEDGMENTS

*N*o book could be written about the unique phenomenon known as McDonald's without acknowledging the contributions of two men: Ray Kroc, the founder whose vision created the company, and Fred Turner, the "architect" of the McDonald's system we know today.

Special thanks to our CEO, Jim Skinner, for encouraging me to write this book, and to Jack Daly, senior vice president of Corporate Relations, for serving as my executive sponsor.

I would also like to acknowledge the people who paved the way by being the pioneers, the first to travel where no one else had ventured. These include our first franchisee, Art Bender in California; our first female franchisee, Lillian McMahon in Michigan; our first African American franchisee, Herman Petty in Illinois; our first Hispanic franchisee, Henry Garcia in California; and our first Asian franchisee, Ted Tongson in Texas. They were the pathfinders who opened the doors of opportunity for so many others after them.

I want to thank my current staff members—Gus Viano and Kevin Bradley—for their steadfast support in carrying the torch of inclusion and diversity throughout the system, shedding light as they go. My special appreciation goes to Lynda DuBovi for her patience and persistence in helping to schedule the interviews that are the core of this book. And a special thanks is extended to all those who have served the cause as part of our department through the years.

In addition, acknowledgment is due to all my colleagues across the country and around the world, my fellow diversity leaders who are working so diligently every day to make inclusion and diversity an integral part of the companies and organizations they serve.

For every interview we did to develop this book, we thought of a dozen more people who could have contributed to our story. I only wish we had had the time to talk to everyone who has been part of this inspiring development of diversity within McDonald's, because our success was clearly an effort by all of us.

I sincerely thank those employees, franchisees, and suppliers—past and present—who so graciously gave us their time and shared their recollections on the evolution of diversity at McDonald's. These include Ernie Adair, Annis Alston, Rita Alborez-Pozniak, Ralph Alvarez, Jose Armario, Bob Beavers, Chris Beck-McKay, Monica Boyles, Ron Brown, Jerry Calabrese, Susan Chrisman, Marge Cooke, Dick Crawford, Don Crosby, Ron Damper, Lee Dunham, Richard Ellis, Steven Eng, Tim Fenton, Janice Fields, Rich Floersch, Henry Garcia, Karen Garcia, Rosemary Garcia, J.C. Gonzalez-Mendez, Maura Havenga, Denis Hennequin, Luis Hernandez, Mel Hopson, Fran Jones, Glen Kikuchi, Bonnie Kos, Victor Lim, Johanne Luth, Roberto Madan, Paula Marshall, Raymond Mines, Herman Petty, Ed Rensi, Rogercarole Rogers, Vivian Ross, Malou Roth, Steve Russell, Catherine Sanchez, Ed Sanchez, Gloria Santona, Stan Stein, Don Thompson, Mike Thompson, Isabelle Villasenor, Reggie Webb, Cosmo Williams, and Marilyn Wright. Finally, I also want to thank Arthur Miller, who helped conduct our interviews and provided invaluable editorial assistance in putting this book together, and to my colleagues Eric Gallender, Susan Clark McBride, and Lisa McComb, who made certain from both a communications and a legal perspective that every word in and aspect of this book are accurate and appropriate reflections of the McDonald's diversity story and the McDonald's brand—and who also were instrumental in bringing this story to others. It is our collective hope that, in doing so, we help make the world a better place.